CW00683717

Shinpiden: Reiki Master Teacher Manual

By Taggart King

Published by Pinchbeck Press

www.pinchbeckpress.com
Email: taggart@reiki-evolution.co.uk

ISBN 978-0-9563168-2-0

3

Introduction

Welcome to Reiki Mastership, and the start of another journey of self-discovery! Maybe you are attending one of our live Master courses, maybe you are taking your Master degree through home study; either way, you have an exciting journey ahead of you!

Shortly you will have the knowledge necessary to attune others at First Degree, Second Degree and Master level, but please do not think about attuning 'the public' until at least three full months have passed because you need to allow time for things to settle down following your own attunements, you need to practise the connection rituals until the procedures are second nature, and you need to spend time deciding what you are going to teach and how you are going to teach it. You can attune your family and friends as soon as you like though!

Unfortunately, when you become a Reiki Master you are Master of nothing: you have simply begun a long and interesting journey. You are not suddenly endowed with infinite wisdom and esoteric knowledge: you have to work at it! So why the title 'Master'? I would prefer to be called a teacher. Maybe you are called a Master because it is not you that has mastered Reiki, but Reiki that has mastered you! Maybe you have been put in contact with the 'master' within: the higher self, or the divine spark that resides in us all.

Just like at First and Second Degree level, you have been given a new ladder to climb. This time it is a very long ladder indeed, but you are still starting your journey on the bottom rung. There is a long way to climb, and how far you travel is down to you: how much you work with the energy, how much you develop yourself.

As with the previous levels, over the next few weeks you are likely to go through a further period of detoxification and cleansing. You may notice some emotional ups and downs as the increased levels of Reiki flow through you, during your treatment of others and during your regular self-treatments. Maybe you will see things in Technicolor for a while, or be filled with an expansive love for everyone and everything. Beyond that, Reiki will continue to make long-lasting positive changes in your life, it will affect your worldview and clarify your priorities for the better. Attuning others will also lead to further periods of cleansing and clearing out at all levels.

Now that you are being attuned at Reiki Master level, the best advice I can give you is to work with the new energies until you become thoroughly familiar with them, work on yourself, and empower yourself regularly. As you know, practice helps to clear and strengthen the channels through which Reiki flows. You are likely to become more intuitive, and the more regularly you make yourself open to intuition the faster this will develop. Experiment with your intent and intuition to see what is possible and discover how far you can push such things.

Make yourself a student of Reiki: I do not have all the answers. Read books, but do not believe everything you read. Try things out for yourself and test them to see if they are effective or valid. Find your own way.

About Your Master Course Materials

Like most people who take Reiki Mastership, my original manuals given to me by Diane Whittle contained Western attunement instructions, together with some information about the Usui Master symbol and the 'Tibetan' symbols, and a few other bits and pieces: Antahkaranas, the Microcosmic Orbit meditation, Reiki Psychic sSurgery and Healing attunements.

The numbered attunement instructions have been retained in more or less their original form (point 1... point 2... etc), though I have added all the summary sheets, flow charts, drawings, photo guides and extra descriptions to make the process easier to understand. I have also retained the antahkarana etc. information, included for your interest, though I do not use these approaches myself and cannot recommend them. The Master manual I received originated with Simon Treselyan, and from William Rand before him in terms of most of the information contained in the materials I was given.

I was not taught very much at all about the practical use of the symbols when carrying out treatments, so I have added a great deal to this information, concentrating on the practical use of these and other new symbols, and I have discussed my view of the symbols and their associated energies, though I do not want to overemphasise the use of symbols since I believe that they have assumed an unnecessary importance within the world of Reiki.

All the sections about the original system that Mikao Usui taught, the Reiki kotodama, Reiju empowerments, Distant connections, self-empowerments, and the use of Intuition and Intent are written by me.

Reiki is a tradition that is passed on from master to student, the student becomes a master and passes it on to others and so on. The next two pages show your Reiki lineage as far back as Mikao Usui, the originator of Reiki, and his photograph.

Acknowledgements

I would like to thank Diane Whittle, a lovely lady, for taking the time, trouble and care to introduce me to Reiki at all levels. Diane taught myself and my fellow students with gentle humour, wisdom and compassion and provided me with a solid foundation to build on. My Reiki Master attunements in the woods and on the beach in Suffolk were something very special!

During my travels throughout the UK and Europe, teaching the methods of Mikao Usui's original system, I had the honour to meet and share knowledge and experiences with many talented and experienced Reiki teachers. It would be difficult to list them all, but in particular I am grateful to Carly Horbowiec from Holland and Chris Deefholts from Oxfordshire for giving me the benefit of their wisdom and experience. I am also indebted to Frank Arjava Petter, Chetna Koyabashi, and Fiona McCallion for introducing me to Japanese-style Reiki.

In particular I need to single out Chris Marsh for thanks: the person who finally led me to real Usui Reiki by providing me with patient training over several years and offering me insights into Mikao Usui's original system, sharing things that I could not have obtained anywhere else in the world.

I would like to thank the hundreds of students who have been through my Reiki courses, who have taught me so much, and I would like to thank Margaret Craig for her help in reading through the text of this new manual and providing me with invaluable feedback.

With best wishes,

Taggart King
5 Rose Lane, Pinchbeck, Spalding, Lincolnshire PE11 3RN
Tel: 0845 458 3004, or 01775 722082
email: taggart@reiki-evolution.co.uk
Web: www.reiki-evolution.co.uk

Your Reiki Lineages

All Reiki practitioners can trace their 'spiritual lineage', following a trail of Reiki teachers back to the originator of Reiki, Mikao Usui. Apparently the Reiki etiquette is to quote the lineage of the first person that attuned you to Master level as your Reiki lineage, so if someone asks you what your lineage is, then you should quote the list shown below:

If you followed a home study course with Taggart, here is your lineage:	If you attended a Reiki Evolution Live Course, here is your lineage:
Mikao Usui Chujiro Hayashi Hawayo Takata Phyllis LeiFurumoto Florence O'Neal Jerry Farley June Woods Simon Treselyan Marcus Hayward Diane Whittle Taggart King ... your name goes here ...	Mikao Usui Chujiro Hayashi Hawayo Takata Phyllis LeiFurumoto Florence O'Neal Jerry Farley June Woods Simon Treselyan Marcus Hayward Diane Whittle Taggart King ... your teacher's name goes here ... ... your name goes here ...

I have various other Reiki lineages, where I have received attunements and informal training from several Reiki teachers in Europe, all variations on Mrs Takata's "Western" style of Reiki. I have also trained in more Japanese-style Reiki with Frank Arjava Petter and I have been taught various techniques that Reiki Master Hiroshi Doi has presented in the West.

One lineage of special note involves my having received empowerments and instruction from Chris Marsh; these empowerments pass on the energy of Usui Sensei through the intermediary of a Tendai Buddhist nun – Suzuki San - who trained with Usui and is now over 100 years old; I received ongoing training from Chris for several years. This would be the most direct transmission:

Mikao Usui
Suzuki San
Chris Marsh
Taggart King

Below I detail, for your interest, a 'family tree' of Reiki teachers whose energy has contributed to my practice of Reiki.

In the following family tree there are some "Usui-Tibetan" lineages, and also some European lineages where I have received attunements and informal training; on the right of the family tree you will see two Japanese energy lines that are outside the standard Hayashi-Takata lineage that most people in the Reiki world have.

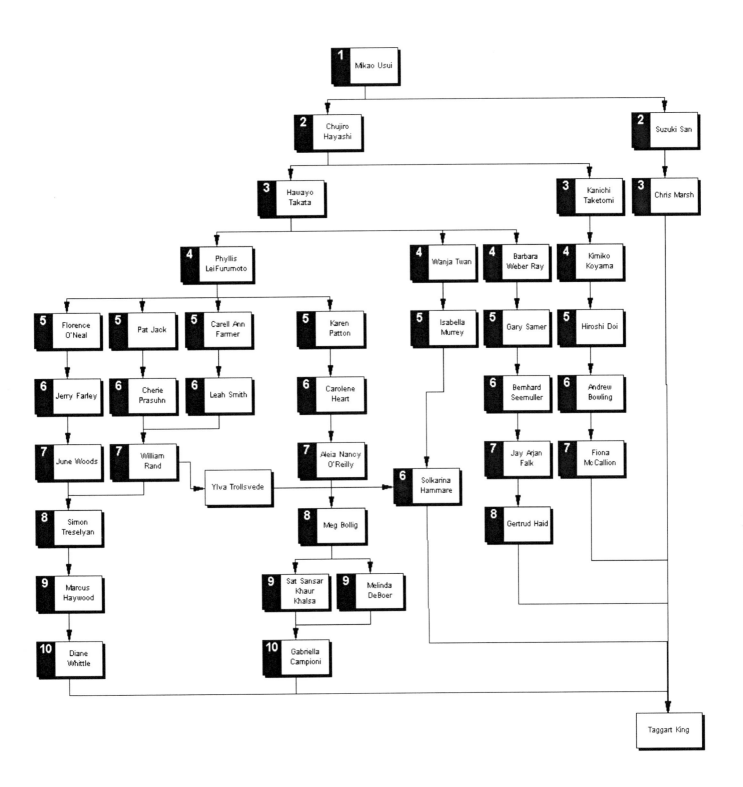

Picture of Mikao Usui

Mikao Usui 1865 - 1926

Overview of the Course

 Master Course Audio CD Number 1 - track #1

Below you can see a diagram showing the main areas covered on this Master / Teacher course. If you are attending one of our live courses then these are the main themes that you will be thinking about and working with during your extensive pre-course practice and on the two-day live course; if you are following our Master / Teacher home study course then during the stages of your course we will again be thinking about and working on these areas.

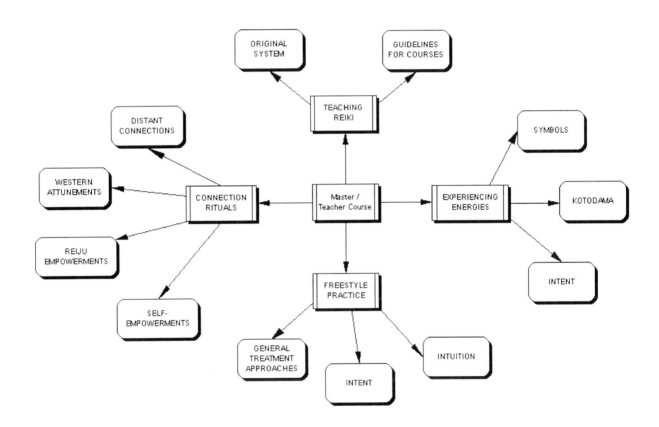

Most Master / Teacher courses deal with western attunements and perhaps not very much beyond that. You **will** be learning how to carry out Western attunements because every other Reiki Master in the world knows how to 'attune', but we will also learn the Reiju empowerments used by Usui Sensei's surviving students, and you'll probably choose to use empowerments on any Reiki1 or Reiki2 courses that you teach. We will also explore distant connections and self-empowerments, both topics that don't seem to be covered on most Master courses either.

But Reiki Mastership shouldn't just be about connection rituals, important though they are. So we are going to be focusing on experiencing different energies and learning how to use these energies in practice when working on ourselves or on other people. We will do this by using symbols - the "Tibetan" and the Usui Master symbols, and various other symbols - and by using the Reiki kotodama, Shinto mantras that predate the use of symbols within Reiki and which were the method used by the majority of Usui Sensei's students. And carrying on with the 'treatment' theme, whether of ourselves of other people, we will consider some ways of moving beyond our self-imposed limitations, by exploring the possibilities of intent and intuition.

Finally, since you may well decide to teach Reiki at some stage, we will also be offering some helpful suggestions and guides, and resources, that will get you off to a good start if and when you decide to start running your own Reiki courses.

As we go through the various stages of the course, we should keep in mind how Mikao Usui taught, and what he taught, and we can see how we can duplicate the original practices, or echo the original practices, within our practice of Reiki.

Using the Course Audio CDs and DVD

Audio CDs

This course is accompanied by two Audio CDs which focus you on the main points of the course and which should be listened to in conjunction with the corresponding sections of the course manual, rather than just being listened to in their entirety. You will learn more effectively if you use audio and visual learning together. In the manual you will find a little icon showing you that there is an audio track to listen to. The icon looks like this:

Below you can read the track listings for both the audio CDs:

Reiki Master / Teacher Course Audio CD # 1: "Commentary"

1	Welcome	2.42
2	The Original System	5.18
3	Experiencing Energies	2.56
4	Symbols and Treatments	8.28
5	The Kotodama	5.26
6	Intent	7.10
7	Intuition	4.02
8	Non-Reiki techniques	10.09
9	Reiju empowerments	9.37
10	Western attunements	6.34
11	Thoughts on Usui System	1.41
12	Teaching Reiki	5.29

Total Running Time   69.32m

Reiki Master / Teacher Course Audio CD # 2: "Instructions"

1	Reiju empowerment instructions	8.20
2	Reiki2 attunement instructions	16.36
3	Frequency Scale meditation instructions	8.16
4	Reiji ho instructions	7.40

Total Running Time   *40.52m*

DVD

This course is accompanied by a 30 minute DVD which shows you how to carry out Reiju empowerments and Second Degree attunements and which should be watched in conjunction with the corresponding sections of the course manual. You will learn more effectively if you use the text, images, audio and video sequences together. In the manual you will find a little icon showing you that there is a video sequence to watch. The icon looks like this:

Students' Experiences

In various parts of he manual, you can read the experiences of some of our students who have been working with Master/Teacher course through home study, and who have been giving detailed written feedback by e-mail. We hope that doing this will enhance your experience of the course, whether working at a distance or on a 'live' course.

Whenever a new student gives their feedback, the paragraph will begin with this icon:

The Original System

 Master Course Audio CD Number 1 - track #2

The information that we have about the original system comes from Chris Marsh, via a group of Usui's surviving students who are in contact with him. Arjava Petter has uncovered a few of the component parts, and some of the basic practices of the Gakkai - as passed on by Hiroshi Doi - echo Reiki in its original form. But Gakkai Reiki is not original Usui Reiki, whether it has come to us via Petter or Doi.

The thing that strikes me most about original Usui Reiki is the fact that it is so simple, so elegant, powerful and uncluttered. The system is not bogged down in endless mechanical techniques and complex rituals. The prime focus of Mikao Usui's Reiki is the personal benefits that will come through committing oneself to working with the system, both in terms of self-healing and spiritual development. Reiki was a path to enlightenment. Healing others was a minor aspect of the system, not emphasised, not focused upon; it was simply something that you could do if you followed Usui's system.

Original Usui Reiki involves committing yourself to carrying out daily energy exercises, treating yourself (a range of approaches were available) and receiving spiritual empowerments on a regular basis. You learned to work with meditations or ancient Shinto mantras that represent different aspects of the energy, and you did this to further your self-healing and spiritual development; these mantras could also be used when treating others. There were very few treatment techniques and the focus was very much on intuition; symbols did not enter into the process for the vast majority of Usui Sensei's students and were only introduced for the Imperial Officers in about 1923; Usui had been teaching his system since at least 1915.

Original Usui Reiki gives all of us the chance to maximise our Reiki potential. We can practice exercises that make us a strong clear channel for Reiki; we can learn to 'become' two important energies, and to experience 'oneness'. And when we treat others, we can learn to open to intuition so that the energy moves our hands to just the right places to treat in each person we work on. Simple. Elegant. Powerful.

A Few Revelations

Let's get three revelations out of the way to begin with:

1. Usui's system wasn't called Reiki
2. Usui's system wasn't about treating people
3. Usui's system didn't use symbols

Usui's System wasn't Called Reiki

The first revelation about original Usui Reiki is that it was not called 'Reiki', in fact Usui's system had no name. Usui seems to have referred to the system as either 'My system' or 'Method to Achieve Personal Perfection'. His students seem to have referred to the system as 'Usui Teate' or 'Usui Do'. The word Reiki appears in the Reiki precepts, but the word 'Reiki' there seems to mean 'a system that has been arrived at through a moment of enlightenment', or 'a gift of satori'. The name 'Reiki' came later, and may have been used first when the naval officers, his less-experienced students, set up the Usui Reiki Ryoho Gakkai after Usui's death. Interestingly, the word Reiki is pronounced "Lay-key" in Japanese.

The teachings that are coming from Usui's surviving students have been referred to as 'Usui Teate' by Chris Marsh and his associate Andrew Bowling, and you may come across this phrase. The word 'teate' should be pronounced 'tee-ah-tay' with emphasis on the first and last syllables. Teate means 'hand healing' or 'hand application', and there is a hundreds of years old tradition of Japanese hand healing techniques that work on he recipient's chi, perhaps similar to QiGong healing techniques.

Usui's System wasn't about Treating People

The next revelation is that the purpose of Usui's method was to achieve satori, to find one's spiritual path, to heal oneself. Usui's system was not really about treating others. Treating others was not emphasised; it was not focused upon; it was a side issue. Usui's system was a spiritual system and his teachings in terms of treating others amounted to "you can do this". Some students were taught some standard hand positions to use when treating the head, and some weren't. The approach was basically intuitive, and any suggested hand-positions were a stopgap. With time the students would move on to treat intuitively, or would carry out 'intention' healings, where they would connect to the recipient and the healing would take place during whatever period was appropriate. Once the initial connection was made, the healing could take place no matter what the 'healer' then went on to do: there was no need to concentrate on the recipient. The initial connection/intention was the thing that led to the healing taking place.

Usui's System didn't use Symbols

As far as the vast majority of Usui Sensei's students are concerned, the system did not involve the use of symbols: they were never taught to use symbols and they were not attuned to symbols. What we refer to as the Reiki symbols were introduced by Usui Sensei and his senior student Eguchi as a quick way of depicting the energies, introduced for the benefit of the Imperial officers who approached Usui in order to learn a hands-on healing system that they could use within the Japanese military. Even then, Usui Sensei did not attune the Imperial Officers to the symbols: they were simply a visual focus that was used to elicit/invoke a particular energy. The other students had used either meditations or chanted Shinto mantras to learn to experience or become a particular energy or a state.

Origins of Usui's System

The system was rooted in Tendai Buddhism, Shintoism and Shugendo (mountain asceticism). Tendai Buddhism (a form of mystical Buddhism) provided spiritual teachings and spiritual empowerments, Shintoism contributed methods of controlling and working with the energies, and Shugendo provided the precepts on which Usui based his own. Usui had a strong background in both kiko (energy cultivation) and a martial art with a strong Zen flavour (Yagyu Shinkage Ryu), and he also took Soto Zen training for a while, and these studies may have contributed in some way to the system that he developed, and certainly contributed to his own spiritual development.

The system was based on living and practising the Reiki principles; that was the hub of the whole thing. The vast majority of Usui's students started out as his clients, people who came to him because they wanted something treated. He would routinely give people empowerments (connect them to Reiki) so that they could treat themselves in between appointments with him, and if they wanted to take things further then they could start formal training. The training was rather like martial arts training: you had an open-ended commitment to study with Usui, not a fixed-length training course, the teachings were geared towards the student's individual needs, and it was only when the student had developed sufficiently that they were invited to move on to higher levels.

It is important to emphasise that to refer to what Usui Sensei was passing on as 'a system' suggests that there were fixed teachings that were passed on in the same way to all his students. This was not the case: he modified his teachings according to the background and needs of his students, as individuals, so some students were given one set of approaches and worked in one particular way, while others were provided with other approaches. Having said that, here you can read about Usui Sensei's general approaches at each training 'level'...

Overview of What Usui taught

First Degree (Shoden)

First Degree (Shoden) was very simple, and it seems that Usui taught hundreds of people at this level. Shoden was all about opening to the energy through receiving empowerments, it was about cleansing and self-healing.

1. Students would receive Reiju empowerments from Usui Sensei again and again. In fact this continued through all levels.

2. The students would carry out simple energy exercises each day. The exercises taught at first-degree level were Kenyoku and Joshin Kokkyu Ho, which are taught in the Usui Reiki Ryoho Gakkai as part of a longer sequence of exercises called 'Hatsurei ho'.

3. The student would practise self-healing; there were different approaches available, including self-healing meditations.

4. Students would chant and live Usui Sensei's precepts.

5. Students would study some specially selected 'Waka' poems, chosen by Usui because they contained various sacred sounds (kotodama).

6. Students would be introduced to the concept of mindfulness.

In anticipation of moving on to Second Degree level, students would have to focus on developing their awareness of their hara; only when they had successfully defined their hara would they move on to the next level. We will talk about this more later. Students would not treat others at first-degree.

A Little about the Precepts

Everyone who has learned Reiki will have seen the precepts, and they are available in a variety of different forms. There is actually some difference between the precepts that Mikao Usui was teaching and the precepts that are quoted commonly in the West, so perhaps we should start by reading the text of Usui Sensei's version:

> *The secret of inviting happiness through many blessings**
> *The spiritual medicine for all illness*
> *For today only: Do not anger; Do not worry*
> *Be humble*
> *Be honest in your work***
> *Be compassionate to yourself and others*
> *Do gassho every morning and evening*
> *Keep in your mind and recite*

The phrase "many blessings" is likely to refer to Reiju empowerments (the 'attunement' method used by Mikao Usui and the surviving students), so it really means "The secret of inviting happiness through receiving many Reiju empowerments", and of course students who trained with Usui Sensei would receive empowerments again and again throughout their training at all levels.

The phrase "be honest in your work" really means "be honest in your dealings with people".

You will note that there is no precept that exhorts us to "honour our parents, elders and teachers". This seems to have been added to the list, perhaps by Mrs Takata, to make the "list of rules to live by" more acceptable to her American audience.

There has been some speculation about where Mikao Usui's precepts come from. It has been claimed that they originate in a book that was published in Usui's time, and it has been claimed that they are based on the edicts of Mutsuhito, the Meiji Emperor. Certainly it seems that many Tendai and Zen Buddhist teachers were passing on similar principles in Usui Sensei's time.

But we now know that Usui's precepts were his wording of an earlier set of precepts that have been traced back to the early 9th Century, precepts which were used in a Tendai sect of Shugendo with which Usui Sensei was in contact. These earlier precepts were the basic daily practice and rule in Shugendo and are worded as follows:

Do not bear anger
For anger is illusion

Do not be worried
Because fear is distraction

Be true to your way and your being

Show compassion to yourself and others

Because this is the centre of Buddhahood

These earlier precepts offer more detail, and they are said to be a way of addressing aspects of the Buddhist eight-fold path, but in a more simplified form. The precepts were the baseline, the foundation of Usui Sensei's teachings, and it was thought that individual could achieve as much spiritual development by following the precepts as could be achieved by carrying out all the energy exercises.

The principles really are the 'hub' of the whole system.

Second Degree (Okuden)

Second Degree (Okuden) was split into two levels (Zenki and Kouki). Perhaps 70 students reached Zenki, with 30 of these reaching Kouki level. Second-degree was all about strengthening your ability as a channel, becoming familiar with some specific energies and a particular state of mind, and receiving spiritual teachings.

You became a stronger channel for Reiki by receiving Reiju empowerments on a regular basis, and by practising energy exercises. Reiju continually reinforced your connection to the source and allowed you to grow spiritually. You would work on that renewed connection by doing daily energy exercises which took a different form from those carried out at first-degree.

The Spiritual teachings introduced at Second Degree level involved studying Buddhist sutras, specifically the Lotus sutra, the Heart sutra and the Diamond sutra. The Lotus sutra is the foundation document of Tendai Buddhism. Though one source of 'original' information claims that Usui became a Shingon Buddhist, his surviving students insist that he was 'Tendai to the end'. The fact that he was Tendai did not stop him from drawing from other spiritual traditions in Japan though.

Mindfulness would be emphasised more at this level.

Zenki

In the first of the two second-degree levels (Zenki) you would practise 'becoming' the energies that in the West we use ChoKuRei and SeiHeKi to represent: these energies are seen as earth Ki and heavenly Ki by the surviving students. You would do this by practising various meditations over many months, or by meditating on sacred sounds, or maybe a bit of both approaches. You learned to 'become' these energies over an extended period of time in order to move along your path to enlightenment, and to promote self-healing. This process was not rushed, since you had to learn to 'become' the energies fully, one energy at a time.

Students would have worked with each aspect of the energy for maybe 6-9 months before moving on, so it was a slow process.

The sacred sounds that you used to further your self-healing and spiritual development could also be used to treat others, and students might do some treatments at this level, though it was a bit of a sideline to the main thrust of the system. Treatments might be based on a few simple hand positions that were used on the head, though this was not taught to all students, and the focus was very much on intuition in terms of hand-placement and in terms of what energy - if any - you emphasised during the treatment. You will already have read above about the use of 'intention' treatments by Usui's students.

The sacred sounds, called 'Kotodama' (or 'Jumon' if referred to from a Buddhist perspective), come from Shintoism, the indigenous religion of Japan. This is really ancient stuff. This takes us back to the mists of ancient Japanese history, to a time when the sound of the human voice was said to be able to stop armies, to kill, to heal and to control the weather. There were three kotodama, or jumon, taught at second degree, representing the three energies that in the West we use the symbols to represent.

The two energies that were introduced at Okuden Zenki and had to be fully integrated before you moved on to Okuden Kouki.

Kouki

At the second of the two second-degree levels (Kouki) you would be introduced to the concept of oneness, one of the goals of the system, and learn through meditations, and/or the use of a Kotodama, to fully experience oneness. Distance healing is an expression of oneness, and students would have realised that they could do this easily.

In fact treating others is an expression of oneness too!

Treatment Techniques

All the other 'Usui' techniques that are practised by the Usui Reiki Ryoho Gakkai (the Japanese association that carries Usui's name) and have been passed to us through Arjava Petter and Hiroshi Doi are in fact not original 'Usui Teate' techniques, but seem to be mostly Japanese QiGong techniques contained in a QiGong manual that was published in 1927 by the Japanese Navy and issued to all Imperial Officers. No doubt Usui knew of these techniques, because he had practised kiko, but they were not part of his system. You will read later that there might be one or two techniques used in the 'Gakkai that Usui taught only to the naval officers, because they needed extra help with the system.

Meditations

The interesting thing about the meditations that Usui taught to his students is that it was only when the students had become completely familiar with the energies that they were given a 'trigger' to connect to what they already had strongly

21

within them. In the West we use a symbol to connect to an energy that is unfamiliar to us; in Usui's system you became familiar with an energy and then were given a way of triggering it.

No symbols entered into Usui's system for most of his students, and thus the empowerments (connection rituals) do not use symbols either; why would they, since Usui's system was up and running long before he introduced symbols for the benefit of Dr Hayashi and the other naval officers in 1923. Usui seems to have taught his system as early as 1915, maybe even earlier.

Master levels (Shinpiden and Shihan)

The Master levels (Shinpiden and Shihan) involved receiving further spiritual teachings, receiving Reiju and other 'higher' empowerments, and learning how to empower yourself. You were introduced to a further kotodama, and you practised a whole series of meditations, or energy exercises, that built on each other and were designed to move you further along your spiritual path and closer and closer to your own satori.

Satori is not the same as the Sanskrit 'nirvana' or spiritual bliss where you experience unity with the divine; it is not a one-time once-and-for-all experience. Satori is a moment of recognition, when you have a flash of insight that changes something in a fundamental way. It would come through a long period of meditation; it is something that you have to work at, by getting rid of your 'baggage'.

There seem to be at least two other 'higher level' Master empowerments. One of them has no name and the other is called 'bringing in the light'. I received both of these empowerments in February 2001, and the first made me feel sick and made my legs go wobbly. Someone fainted when receiving this empowerment, and another person lost control of their legs for a while, so I think I got off lightly.

It is only possible to carry out these empowerments once you have practised certain meditations for a long period of time.

Eventually, near the end of your Master training, you learned how to perform Reiju and other 'higher' empowerments. This may have been described as 'Shihan' level rather than 'Shinpiden' (mystery teachings). The system was open-ended though: you never completed it; it was a lifetime journey. It was about defining and finding your place cosmically.

It took as long as it took, through continued practice.

Experiencing Energies

 Master Course Audio CD Number 1 - track #3

Introduction

We know that in the original system Usui Sensei's students were introduced to the energies of earth ki and heavenly ki at Second Degree level, and some students moved on to experience a state of oneness. This was done through meditation, or through chanting kotodama (Shinto mantras). These energies had to be fully assimilated before the student moved on, so for example a student would spend 6-9 months working with earth ki, to fully 'become' that energy, before moving on to spend a similar amount of time working with heavenly ki. The majority of the Second Degree students would have stopped there, and only a small number would have moved on to that later part of Second Degree, where they would learn to fully embrace a state of oneness.

The energies were focused upon because the student needed to get to grips with these energies to further their self-healing and their spiritual development, not because the energies were useful when treating others, though the energies are of course useful in that respect. Treating others was not what Usui's system was all about, and so the energies were introduced because of what they would do for the student in terms of their self-healing and spiritual development.

Later on you will be finding out about the Reiki kotodama, and using these ancient mantras to experience the energies of earth ki and heavenly ki, and a state of oneness, but this is not the way that Reiki is generally taught or experienced in the West. Western Reiki is all about symbols, being attuned to symbols and working with symbols, sometimes on yourself or more commonly on other people. There has been a belief that you cannot channel Reiki without being 'attuned' to the Reiki symbols in some way, and that the Reiki symbols taught at Second Degree, for example, will not work for you until you have been specifically 'attuned' to them.

The new information from Japan has turned such beliefs upside down, because we now know how to connect people to Reiki without using attunements or symbols - by using Reiju empowerments - and we now know that you do not need to be attuned to a symbol - whatever that means - in order for it to work for you. For a symbol to work for you, you just need to be connected to Reiki, and we can now achieve that in a symbol-free fashion (by using Reiju empowerments)!

The Reiki symbols were introduced into Reiki late in Usui's life. Usui and his senior student Eguchi introduced them jointly, and they were introduced for the Imperial Officers. The Imperial Officers approached Usui wanting to be taught a simple treatment technique that could be used in the Imperial Navy: Usui was a well-known healer in his time. The Imperial Officers were not so interested in working on the self and they did not have the time to go through the various exercises that were being carried out by the other students, so the symbols were introduced as a quick way of depicting the energies in a treatment context.

But the symbols still depicted earth ki, heavenly ki and a state of oneness. Usui did not 'attune' the Imperial Officers to the symbols – he did not attune anyone to anything, since the Imperial Officers developed attunements after his death. They would have received empowerments from Usui in the same fashion as the other students – and the symbols were given to them (just like the kotodama were given) as a tool to use to experience a particular energy.

These symbols came via Dr Hayashi and Mrs Takata to the West, and many ways of working with symbols have been developed in different lineages. A lot of these approaches tend to be complicated: the idea of CKR being a 'power' symbol that you have to put on top of other symbols to 'empower' them, for example, and the idea of mixing symbols all the time, sometimes in complicated sequences. As Chris Marsh said to me, "this is not a very Japanese way of doing things!"

All these approaches will do **something**, of course, but they have nothing to do with what Usui was teaching, and they do not allow the practitioner to get to grips with the essence of earth ki and heavenly ki, for example, because the student is taught to mix the symbols all the time.

So most people within the world of Reiki will not know what SHK energy feels like, or what CKR energy feels like, because they have never had the chance of working with the energies individually and meditating on them.

The symbols, and the kotodama, are there to allow us to get to grips with different energies, or different aspects of the energy. Earth ki and heavenly ki are there right from the beginning, at First Degree level, in the energy we are channelling, but the symbols or kotodama allow us to focus our attention more clearly on one aspect of the energy, they 'flag up' an energy to us, or elicit an energy within us, so we can recognise it and work with it.

Below you will be introduced to some new symbols. I need to make it clear that only one of these symbols was present in the original system: the Usui Master Symbol, the Usui DaiKoMyo (DKM). This symbol had always been there in Usui's system as a symbolic representation of 'the key to the light' (the key to the system) but it was not **used** by students (in the way that we understand symbols being 'used'), certainly not until the Imperial Officers arrived.

All the other symbols you will see below are non-Reiki symbols from various sources, and it is up to you whether you choose to use them in your practice. They are included in this manual and on this course mainly to help you to realise how sensitive you are to the energies, and how you can learn to experience different 'energy signatures' through using graphical representations of the energy.

Once you are connected to Reiki then **any** symbol seems to push the energy in a particular way so, whether or not you are 'attuned' to a symbol, it will focus the energy in a particular way for you. So if you want to explore the energies used in other Reiki-style systems like, for example, Karuna or Seichem, then you can do this now without being attuned to these systems, simply by using and meditating on the Karuna or Seichem symbols.

Symbols

 Master Course Audio CD Number 1 - track #4

Symbols are an essential component of Western Reiki, since they were an integral part of the system that Dr Hayashi passed on to Mrs Takata. We know that symbols were not part of Usui's original system: he used kotodama and meditations to represent the energies, and the Reiki symbols were only taught to a few of his Masters: the naval officers and one of the surviving students it seems.

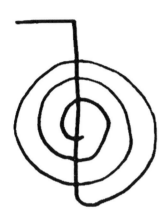

If we accept that Reiki connects us to 'the source' then we have it all already - all aspects of the energy are already there, and symbols are useful sometimes because they connect us, or allow us to focus more effectively, on one particular aspect of the energy. However, there are other ways of doing this, for example the use of intent; intent is more important than we realise and we will be dealing more with the use of intent later.

Through familiarity with the energies that the symbols represent (or that the kotodama represent, for that matter) we can actually move beyond the symbols and access their energies direct.

But there are no shortcuts: we can only move beyond the symbols to access their energies direct, in a deep and effective way, if we have become thoroughly familiar with those energies. We can do this by meditating on the energies, by assimilating them, by 'becoming' those energies. That was the original approach. A suitable symbol meditation is included in the Second Degree manual, and is reproduced again later.

I am not really a fan of endless symbols, so it is ironic that I have ended up teaching quite a few on the Master course! The only symbol introduced in this Manual that has anything to do with Usui Reiki in its original form is the Usui Master symbol, which, together with CKR, SHK and HSZSN, made up the four symbols that Usui had in his later system. They correspond to the energies that lie behind the four kotodama used in Usui's system.

When the symbols were taught in the West, to begin with people were not allowed to take home 'hard copies': they had to burn the pieces of paper that they practised on during the course, and then had to reproduce them from memory. When a group of Mrs Takata's Masters got together after her death and showed each other their symbols, there were marked differences. Some people say that this shows that Mrs Takata changed and modified the symbols for different students; more likely I believe that the students just remembered and reproduced them differently, and over time 'Chinese whispers' has led the symbols to change even further over time.

A few years ago a Western Reiki Master called Dave King (no relation) from Canada made contact with an elderly Reiki Master called Tatsumi, who had been taught Reiki by Dr Hayashi. Dave copied the symbols that he was shown in Tatsumi's notes, and you can see three of these symbols alongside the text you were reading above!

It is interesting to see the 'evolution' of the Reiki symbols over time. Tatsumi's version of DKM (the Master symbol) is here (left).

To the right is the Master symbol that I teach (drawn by Eri Takase, Master Calligrapher).

They are quite similar, which is reassuring. Though I don't think we should get too worked up about whether our symbols are 100% accurate, I think that if you can use a symbol that is closer to what seems to be its original form, then that is probably a good idea.

When I first trained as a Reiki Master, my version of the Master symbol was quite different, and you can see below how the symbol has evolved from the Tatsumi version (left) into what I was first taught (right) ...

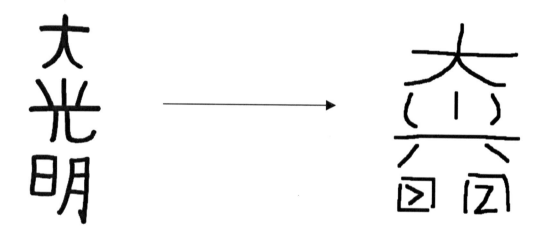

In the rest of this 'Symbols' section of the Manual, I start by recapping some information about the three Second Degree Symbols, and then I have split the remaining symbols into four different categories, based on their usage/effects:

1. Soul Healing
2. Producing Balance
3. Focusing on Thoughts and Emotions
4. Dealing with Karma.

The most important of these symbols are the two 'Master' symbols, the 'balance' symbols are quick and useful, and the others should be used intuitively: don't plan to use them, but just 'go with the flow' and use them when you have a strong feeling that you ought to. Otherwise you will end up with a very cluttered practice!

Second Degree Symbols

Cho Ku Rei

ChoKuRei is said to mean 'by divine decree' and has correspondences in Shintoism, where the phrase is used as an order (e.g. 'let there be sunshine… ChoKuRei'). It is also found in Tendai Buddhism, with an indefinite spiral.

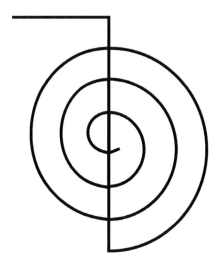

ChoKuRei is a symbol that depicts a particular energy, and corresponds to the 'Focus' kotodama. This kotodama produces earth energy. Ki that emanates from the earth is heavy, firm and powerful. It grounds the body and mind, giving mental and physical strength. Earth Ki is forest green in colour and links the body to the earth. This energy can be seen as a physical healing energy, an energy that reminds you who you are.

Students were introduced to this energy at Second Degree because of the effects that this energy would produce in furthering the student's self-healing and spiritual development.

ChoKuRei can be used when giving treatments, and within the world of Western Reiki the symbol has connotations of space-clearing and protection. In original Usui Reiki there is no conception of the 'focus' energy being a 'power' energy, so the idea that **ChoKuRei** represents a 'power' symbol that you place over other symbols to 'empower' them seems to be a Western misconception or misunderstanding: the main effect of the 'focus' kotodama is to produce physical healing, it is earth Ki, and **ChoKuRei** represents the same energy.

Using ChoKuRei when giving Reiki treatments

Cho Ku Rei produces a low frequency energy, and its main purpose is physical healing.

When the symbol is drawn over the body, the effect is twofold:

1. the symbol boosts the flow of energy through your hands
2. the symbol gears the energy towards physical healing

In practice, **ChoKuRei** can be drawn anywhere on the body where there is a need for physical healing, so you could draw it over your hand(s) when treating a 'hot spot', e.g. an area of local injury or an arthritic knee. Ideally you will work with this energy intuitively, so you emphasise this energy during treatments when you have a strong feeling that you ought to. The easiest way of focusing your attention on the symbol is to have the symbol up in the air above you as you treat, representing the source of the energy, rather than drawing or visualising it over your hands.

Sei He Ki

SeiHeKi is found all over Japan in its calligraphic form, and can be found in India and Tibet also, in Buddhist temples. The symbol we use is a line version of the Japanese symbol, which in itself is a Japanese version of a letter from the Sanskrit alphabet, the sound of which, when chanted, is said to produce 'mental spring cleaning'.

SeiHeKi is a symbol that depicts a particular energy, and corresponds with the 'Harmony' kotodama. This kotodama produces heavenly energy. Ki that emanates from heaven is light, etherical (relates to the etheric body) and is passive. Heavenly Ki increases intuition, psychic ability (psychic awareness) and mental focus. Heavenly Ki is golden in colour. The harmony kotodama is heavenly Ki, and SeiHeKi represents the same energy.

Students were introduced to this energy at Second Degree because of the effects that this energy would produce in furthering the student's self-healing and spiritual development.

SeiHeKi can be used when giving treatments, of course, and in the West this symbol is commonly called the mental/emotional symbol.

Using SeiHeKi when giving Reiki treatments

Sei He Ki generates a higher frequency energy than Cho Ku Rei, and is used to balance the mental and emotional planes. Usui's surviving students describe this energy as heavenly energy, heavenly Ki, an energy that makes a link with the spiritual, drawing the two energies into harmony. When the symbol is drawn over the body, the effect is twofold:

1. the symbol boosts the flow of energy through your hands
2. the symbol gears the energy towards mental balancing and emotional release

The effects of SeiHeKi are less noticeable to your hands, because they resonate at a higher frequency than ChoKuRei, and the energy feels more fine and delicate; but it is still as 'powerful'.

The effects that SeiHeKi produces are wide-ranging. The symbol will deal with stress, tension, anxiety, sleeplessness, restlessness and traumas. It will help a person to deal with anger, heal sorrow and release emotional blocks, and resolves deep-seated emotional problems: unresolved issues that grind away in the background without being dealt with. The symbol can also be used to modify and improve habits and personality traits.

In practice, **SeiHeKi** can be drawn over these areas:

1. head
2. heart
3. solar plexus

These are the main mental areas and the main emotional centres. In Traditional Chinese Medicine various emotions are seen as being held in particular organs. For example, anger is held in the Liver, fear is held in the Kidneys, grief is held in the Lungs, joy is held in the Heart and sympathy is held in the Spleen. So one could conceivably use energy from **SeiHeKi** in these areas to deal with these specific emotions, or imbalances associated with them. I would recommend that you let your intuition guide you: if you feel that you ought to use this energy in a particular area then do so, but do not try and treat an emotion in a calculated, academic way. TCM is much more complicated than that!

Hon Sha Ze Sho Nen

It is not completely clear what the meaning of this symbol is, because it is made up of five separate 'kanji'. The kanji have been 'overlapped' so that they produce one big composite character, so for example the bottom part of 'hon' looks like the upper part of 'sha' and so the two are merged to eliminate repetition of the same shapes and lines. The same applies to the bottom part of 'sha' and the top part of 'ze' etc. You can see the 'expanded' version of the symbol in a couple of pages' time, for your information.

Each kanji has a range of meanings that change with context and when combined with other kanji. In 'secret' Shintoism the phrase 'honshazeshonen' means 'man and God are one', but it is not known how this is written. Hiroshi Doi gives the meaning as 'I unite with God'. One interpretation in the West is to give the meaning 'bring wholeness and completion now'.

HonShaZeShoNen is not a symbol that produces energy of a particular frequency – as are **ChoKuRei** and **SeiHeKi**. This symbol allows the Reiki energy to be connected in a particular way: in a way where you do not have to worry about time or distance, and it is an integral part of Reiki practice.

HonShaZeShoNen corresponds with the 'Connection' kotodama. This kotodama does not produce an energy. It produces a state of mind in the practitioner, a state of mind of 'oneness'. Oneness is one of the goals of Usui's system, and chanting this kotodama, as Usui's Shinto students would have done, helps you along this path. A side-effect of oneness, an extrapolation of the idea, is the ability to send Reiki to another person 'at a distance'. But treating another person is an expression of oneness too.

HonShaZeShoNen can be used to send healing energy to someone sitting next to you (without putting your hands on them). You can send Reiki to someone who is the other side of the street, in a different village or town, or in a different continent.

There are other connotations to this energy too. Usui's surviving students describe the associated kotodama as a 'connection' kotodama, so perhaps you might think about using this energy when you can see that someone is resisting an emotional release. Visualise **HSZSN** over the solar plexus so that the emotions are 'connected up' and released. Maybe if you feel that a person needs to express their emotions or their thoughts better, visualise **HSZSN** over the throat-heart-solar plexus, or throat-head, to 'connect' the mental or emotional areas with the communication centre. This need only be done for a few moments; you are not channelling energy in the way that you are with **CKR** and **SHK**.

Perhaps when you start a treatment, and you are resting your hands on someone's shoulders, you might visualise **HSZSN** in your head, and say its name three times, by way of 'connecting' with the person on all levels, or on a deep level.

By guided by your feelings and impressions. Do not do this in a calculated, analytical fashion. Go with the flow and use the symbol when it feels appropriate.

Hon →

Sha →

Ze →

Sho →

Nen →

Soul Healing

The Usui Master symbol

Pronunciation:
Die - **Coe** (Sebastian Coe) - **Mee-Oh**, with emphasis on 'Coe'

Origins and meanings

A number of translations exist for the meaning of this symbol and a number of variations of the symbol itself are in circulation within differing Reiki systems. It appears that all have the same effect in attuning students, but if the symbol is changed too much then the meaning of the symbol changes, and I heard of at least one person in Japan who paid $10,000 to be attuned to a symbol whose meaning was 'big arsehole'!

All things being equal, it is better to be attuned to a symbol that correctly represents the energy associated with it. The symbol given in this manual is as drawn out Eri Takase, Master Calligrapher. Note that all vertical lines are drawn downwards and all horizontal lines are drawn from left to right.

Here are the common translations of the Usui Master Symbol:

- The standard dictionary definition of the secret name of the Master symbol would be 'Great being of the Universe, shine on me, be my friend'.

- The Zen definition, taken from the Encyclopaedia of Eastern Philosophy and Religion, indicates an expression of the true Buddha-nature of man, or the experience of enlightenment. The definition is given as 'Treasure house of the Great Beaming Light'. This would certainly link to Mikao Usui's own reported expression of the energy on Mount Kurama.

- Another more recent definition, and in fact the one used by Hawayo Takata, is 'Praise be to the Great Universal Light of Transcendental Wisdom'.

Interestingly, the DaiKoMyo had always been there in Usui's system, but not as a symbol that was used, not a symbol that you were 'attuned' to. It was a symbol that represented the "key to the light", the key to the system, a representation of the ability to transfer the Reiki ability to another.

This is where the Shugendo connection comes in, according to Chris Marsh, with links to Fudo Myo, a wrathful deity. Fudo Myo is one of the five Myos, or Buddha aspects. Fudo Myo is the guardian of the light, and he wears a medallion with DKM on it: the 'key to the light'.

Here is the latest and most accurate information we have:

The Usui Master symbol and the corresponding empowerment kotodama are related to the Japanese deity Dainichi Nyorai (Mahavairocana, Great Shining One), the Great Buddha of Universal Illumination, Great Sun Buddha, great light of the Universe. Dainichi Nyorai is the embodiment of Illumination (enlightenment) and represents the Universe in its ultimate form, totality and reality. Through his life force he maintains the creation and operation of the Universe and all things emerge from and are nourished by him. Dainichi Nyorai is literally everywhere and everything. All the other Buddhas and Bodhisattvas are various emanations or aspects of his love, compassion, wisdom and other activities.

The core teaching of the Mahavairocana sutra is that Enlightenment is simply 'to know one's mind as it truly is'. The way to achieve this, it says, is to have a mind bent towards enlightenment, to be motivated solely by compassion, and to be expedient in practice to the last.

The corresponding empowerment kotodama represented creative energy, regenerative energy, the energy of rebirth. The idea here is that when Reiju is carried out it connects the recipient to the energy, allowing them to be 'reborn': reborn in the sense of creating a place within that is 'what we originally were', the state within the ovum when we were Divine essence in complete connection to the universe. The energy was the essence of earth and heavenly energy, white light, source, ultimate being.

Uses of the Usui Master Symbol

Attunements

The Usui Master symbol is the 'key' to carrying out Western-style Reiki attunements, as you will see in the descriptions of the attunement methods we use. The symbol can be seen as producing a very high frequency energy that raises the vibrational frequency of the energy system of the recipient.

Treatments

The Usui Master Symbol can be used when carrying out Reiki treatments, though its use would better be restricted to specific situations, and it would not tend to be used routinely. The symbol produces high frequency energy that does not deal directly with the physical, emotional or mental aspects of a person. Rather it works at the level of the soul or spirit, and a Reiki treatment carried out using this symbol could be seen as flooding a person with divine love or divine light. The situations where treatment using the Usui Master Symbol would be appropriate could be as follows:

- Self-destructive behaviour, for example anorexia
- Low self-esteem
- Hate
- Anger

These are all situations where a person is being eaten up inside, deep down, by destructive thoughts and emotions... not just that they are feeling angry or feeling hate, but that they are being destroyed by these emotions. When I have been guided to use this energy, I have given a series of treatments, as follows:

1. a treatment using the energy from **CKR** only
2. a treatment using the energy from **SHK** only
3. a treatment using the energy from the 'Tibetan' **DKM** only
4. a treatment using the energy from the Usui **DKM** only

You seem to be 'peeling back the layers of an onion'. You do not leap in and try to heal at a soul level without first 'touching base' with the more solid layers of being: physical, mental and emotional. By moving on to the 'Tibetan' **DKM** you can see this as clearing and cleansing the soul, this to be followed by flooding the person with Divine light (the Usui **DKM**).

Obviously the most worthwhile method of delivering energy from the Usui Master Symbol is to channel energy from that symbol throughout the course of an entire treatment. Since people have been arguing about the location of the human soul for a very long time, you would not really want to try and direct it to one particular part of the body. You would use the energy for the whole of a treatment. To recap, you would do the following:

> *Visualise a large Usui DaiKoMyo up in the air above you, and say its name three times to empower it. In each hand position, imagine that you are drawing down energy from this symbol, and that the energy is flowing like a cascade, a monsoon or a flood, travelling through your crown, through your shoulders, arms and hands, and out of your hands into the person you are treating. Continue this throughout the course of the whole treatment.*

Tibetan' Master Symbol

Pronunciation (same as Usui Master Symbol):
Die - **Coe** (Sebastian Coe) - **Mee-Oh**, with emphasis on 'Coe'

Although this symbol and the 'Fire Dragon' Symbol are called 'Tibetan', it is unlikely that their origins are strictly Tibetan. The symbols came to the West via Reiki Masters who were initiated into their applications by way of China and Asia, apparently, and it is likely that the symbols are shamanic. The symbols work but they are not traditional Usui symbols. It is fairly certain that an American called Arthur Robertson - said to be the only master student of Iris Ishikuru (Takata's student) - introduced these symbols into Reiki, along with the Antahkaranas too.

The name of the Tibetan Master Symbol is **DaiKoMyo**, the same name as the Usui Master Symbol. My impression is that the Tibetan Master Symbol uses a lower frequency from that of the Usui system. Research into this symbol is said to have shown similarities with Tibetan 'Domo', or clearing of negative energy, rituals. The horn indicated by the first lines provides a receptacle for the positive lightning flash to dispel the negative energy into. The lightning flash also resembles that found in a Kabbalistic ritual for empowerment, apparently.

Use in Attunements

The symbol is primarily used as a cleanser, hence its use with the violet breath as an integral part of our attunement process. The Tibetan Master Symbol can be seen as clearing any blockages to the Usui attunement energy that follows it, it clears a path, opens and protects. The Tibetan Master symbol is not part of all Reiki attunement rituals, only "Usui-Tibetan" rituals. Some Reiki Masters are not given this symbol and so it will not feature in their connection rituals. Clearly, you can attune without using this symbol

Use in Treatments

The Tibetan Master Symbol can be used when carrying out Reiki treatments, though its use is best restricted to specific situations and it would not tend to be used routinely. The symbol produces high frequency energy that does not deal directly with the physical, emotional or mental aspects of a person. Rather it works at the level of the soul or spirit, and is best used in conjunction with the Usui Master Symbol. The symbol produces energy of a frequency less than that achieved by the Usui Master Symbol. Energy derived from this symbol can be seen as cleansing, clearing out, or scouring the soul/spirit, clearing things out of the way ready for energy from the Usui Master Symbol.

The situations where treatment using the Usui Master Symbol would be appropriate are as follows:

- Self-destructive behaviour, for example anorexia
- Low self-esteem
- Hate
- Anger

These are all situations where a person is being eaten up inside, deep down, by destructive thoughts and emotions... not just that they are feeling angry or feeling hate, but that they are being destroyed by these emotions.

When I have been guided to use this energy, I have given a series of treatments, as follows:

1. a treatment using the energy from **CKR** only
2. a treatment using the energy from **SHK** only
3. a treatment using the energy from the 'Tibetan' **DKM** only
4. a treatment using the energy from the Usui **DKM** only

You seem to be 'peeling back the layers of an onion'. You do not leap in and try to heal at a soul level without first 'touching base' with the more solid layers of being: physical, mental and emotional. By moving on to the 'Tibetan' **DKM** you can see this as clearing and cleansing the soul, this to be followed by flooding the person with Divine light (the Usui **DKM**).

Obviously the most worthwhile method of delivering energy from the 'Tibetan' Master Symbol is to channel energy from that symbol throughout the course of an entire treatment, using the 'advanced' technique described in the Reiki Second Degree manual. Since people have been arguing about the location of the human soul for a very long time, you would not really want to try and direct it to one particular part of the body. You would use the energy for the whole of a treatment. To recap, you would do the following:

- Visualise a large Tibetan DaiKoMyo up in the air above you, and say its name three times to empower it.
- Throughout the treatment, imagine that you are drawing down energy from this symbol, and that the energy is flowing like a cascade, a monsoon or a flood, travelling through your crown, through your shoulders, arms and hands, and out of your hands into the person you are treating. Continue this throughout the course of the whole treatment.

Other Uses

The Tibetan Master Symbol can also be used in room clearance, in the same way that **CKR** can be used. This ties in more directly with its origins as a symbol used in rituals to cleanse a space of negative energy.

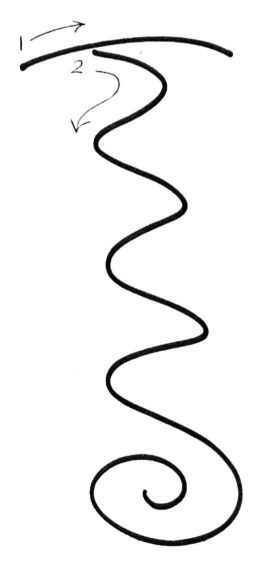

Producing Balance

The Fire Dragon

The serpent symbol is a fairly universal one that seems to resemble Asian correspondences relating to the raising of the 'Kundalini'. The weave of the serpent relates to the seven chakras spiralling into the base or seat of Kundalini. The effect of the Fire Dragon Symbol is as follows:

9

- The symbol opens all seven chakras as necessary, and thus deals with any chakras that might be closed or spinning sluggishly.

- The symbol balances the chakras, thus dealing with any chakras that might be spinning too fast.

- The balancing effect of the symbol seems to be geared to the needs of the individual, rather than producing a 'standard' balance.

This symbol can be used to balance a client's chakras before, during or after treatments. The symbol will only balance the chakras temporarily: it is not an instant 'fix'.

In practice, it is only necessary to use this symbol to open and balance the chakras at the beginning of a treatment: a Reiki treatment on its own will balance the chakras, and so to use the symbol at the end of a Reiki treatment would be unnecessary. By opening and balancing the chakras at the start of a treatment, the patient's energy system is fully receptive to the Reiki energy, and energy does not have to be used in achieving chakra balance before the healing work can be done.

I have used a pendulum to dowse the state of patients' chakras before and after the use of the Fire Dragon symbol, and I can confirm that it does indeed open up the chakras as necessary for each individual patient.

Although I was taught to say 'Fire Dragon, Fire Dragon, Fire Dragon' to myself when I used the symbol, it seems that this is not necessary. Simply draw or visualise the symbol, with the horizontal over the crown, and the 'dragon' running down to the level of the root chakra where it stops and spirals.

This symbol can be used before the patient arrives for his or her treatment: simply imagine the symbol over the person you are going to be treating. I have used a pendulum to dowse this effect, and it works!

There is no name that need be chanted when using this symbol.

You can use this symbol on yourself if you like: visualise it in the air in front of you and then merge it into your body, from crown to root. Notice how you feel.

Channelled Symbols

A few years ago I channelled three symbols: the Spirit Column, the Mental Spiral and the Emotional Butterfly. While I was given some information about their usage at the time that I channelled them, it now seems that they are 12th Century Taoist symbols, according to a Master student of mine who grew up on a Buddhist monastery in Singapore. Please note that I have no way of independently verifying this.

The symbols differ in their use from the standard Reiki symbols in that they do not have an associated name that has to be repeated as a mantra. In this respect their use is more akin to the use of the 'Fire Dragon' symbol, which also does not require the intonation of an associated phrase or mantra.

The story I have so far is that a monk in China caused a serious problem with his karmic field and was given these symbols to cleanse his karmic field following a period of meditation. The symbols had such a profound effect on him that he took the signs from village to village across China. The symbols are now found in Hinduism, Taoism, Zen Buddhism and other forms of Buddhism. They are not written down, but are taught to Buddhist monks by the shape being traced out by hand movements. The originals are kept locked up; they are privileged symbols that are revered.

The Spirit Column

The 'Spirit Column' symbol is used to balance the spiritual, physical and auric field, putting them all in tune with each other. It produces instant balance, and does a great deal more than the Fire Dragon.

For example, I have discovered that this symbol balances one's elements: wood, fire, and earth, metal and water. In practice you could use it at the start and at the end of every treatment.

Though this symbol is not part of Reiki, it seems capable of producing useful effects. Try it out for yourself and see what you notice.

When you draw the symbol, start at the top, with the upper spiral, and move down the page...

You can use this symbol on yourself if you like: visualise it in the air in front of you and then merge it into your body, from crown to root. Notice how you feel.

The symbol will only produce its balancing effects temporarily: it is not an instant 'fix'.

Focusing on Thoughts and Emotions

The Mental Spiral

I am advised that this symbol is as yet incomplete. It works on the mental aspect, but seems to penetrate deeper than SeiHeKi. In use, you would draw/visualise the first part of the symbol over the forehead, and trace the remainder over the crown towards the back of the head, with the recipient on the treatment table in front of you, and you sitting at the head of the table.

Symbolism:

The top spiral represents the higher consciousness. The bottom spiral represents the subconscious.

When you draw the symbol, start with the upper spiral...

The Heart Chakra symbol

The Pronunciation is as follows:

Shi   as in **shi**p
Ka   as in **cu**p
Sei   as in 'say'
Ki   as in 'key'

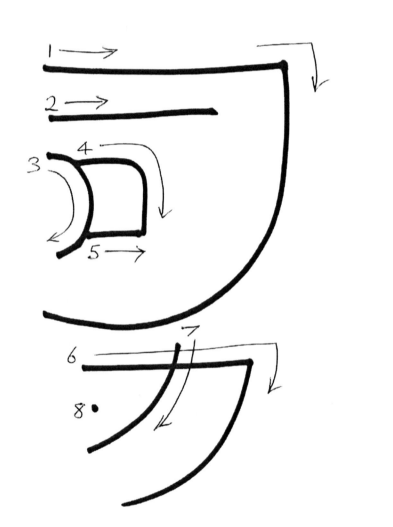

This symbol was taught to me by Jay Arjan Falk and Gertrud Haid, Reiki Masters from Germany and Austria - Jay was the first person to start teaching Reiki Jin Kei Do in Germany, in fact. This 'heart chakra' symbol comes from Barbara Weber-Ray's 'Radiance Technique', from Level 4 of the technique I am told - this is a Master level.

The story behind this is that Weber-Ray was Hawayo Takata's 'senior' student, I believe, and it is claimed that she was taught things by Mrs Takata that she hadn't taught to her other Masters. Mrs Takata had apparently been to see the originator of the Reiki variation called 'Jin Kei Do' as I understand it, and had taken notes, and it is alleged that these notes came to be held by Barbara Weber-Ray after Mrs Takata's death. As I understand it, Weber-Ray then developed her own system using this additional knowledge and Mrs Takata's notes, allegedly, and called her system 'The Radiance Technique' to make a distinction between that and the Reiki that Mrs Takata had taught to her other Masters.

Another contact that I have suggests that this symbol is used in level four of an Eastern lineage of Reiki, though this has not come to us from the group of Usui's surviving students.

The Radiance technique is very expensive, and it was a German man, Gary Samer, who decided to break away from the high charges and make the technique available to ordinary people in Germany. The symbol comes from this source.

The 'herzchakrasymbol' which was given to me comes with the by-line 'Licht und Liebe kommen strahlend aus dem Herzen', which means "Light and Love come flowing out of the heart" and Jay went on to say " ... and connects with all the other hearts". The name of the symbol is 'Shi Ka Sei Ki'. The symbol focuses on the heart, and can be seen as flooding a person with love, according to Jay; it can be used on other places than the heart, too, he says.

My impression is that this symbol produces energy of a specific frequency, and deals with the emotional aspect, allowing a person to be more open to give and receive love, among other things. In conjunction with the 'Mental Spiral' these symbols can be seen as splitting the area dealt with by **SeiHeKi** into two distinct areas - the mental, and the emotional. With practice one would be able to feel the distinctive energies of these symbols, and move beyond the symbols to generate their particular frequencies using direct intent.

The mental spiral could be used over the head, and **ShiKaSeiKi** could be used over the heart particularly, and the solar plexus.

Dealing with Karma

The Emotional Butterfly

This symbol is described as a karmic cleanser. I am advised that it predates the 'Grace' symbol (see later), which is also a karmic cleanser. In practice, you could use the emotional butterfly first, visualising it over the whole body, and then follow this with the 'Grace' symbol a little while later. The symbol would have an effect on the emotional side of things, by making a person alert to the problem that they are storing. The symbol will dig deep, clearing and cleansing the heart Chakra.

Symbolism:

The heart shape represents hearing, and the information that is stored in the mind.

The top circle represents the higher consciousness, storing information that affects the karmic field and the physical body.

The two blobs on the side represent the auric field and the physical body.

For me, a good example of the way that these symbols should be used is exemplified by the experience of one of my Reiki Masters, Janet. See below.

Janet had been treating a lady who had been married and divorced because her first husband had an affair. When Janet was treating her, she was in the process of splitting up with her next partner, who had also had an affair. When Janet was treating her, she had this very strong feeling that she ought to be using the Emotional Butterfly with her, so she visualised the symbol over the lady's chest for a while and let the energy flow.

When the lady returned for the next treatment, she said to Janet "Do you know, for the first time I have actually realised why all this has been happening to me and what I need to move on in my life", which had Janet rushing off to the manual to look up the effects of the symbol: the lady had almost repeated the characteristic of the symbol, which is to allow someone to realise deep down in their heart what they need to do to move on in life.

So we shouldn't use these symbols in a calculating, academic way if we can help it, but bring them into our treatments when we have a strong feeling that this is the right thing to do. Our feelings are in a lot closer contact with our intuition than our head, which gets in the way half the time. Follow your feelings, don't analyse, just go with the flow and do what feels right.

The 'Grace' symbol

By Simon Treselyan

At the end of April 1995 I had the pleasure to be amongst fifteen other Reiki Masters at a retreat in Wales. As with these meetings there are inevitably many reasons for a person being in a certain place at a certain time. This was one of those meetings.

After the retreat had ended and those attending were preparing to go, I was approached by Ian McGarrity. Ian and I attended the same Master course and he had shown himself to be a very advanced soul, treading many paths outside normal experience. Ian was an ex-Royal Marine and we had linked very well during the six months or so we had known each other. Ian drew out for me a symbol, stating that it was a Grace symbol and that he would be interested in my comments.

Ian commented that his sister, Jill Turner, an acclaimed healer and light worker based in Maine, USA, had channelled the symbol. Jill regularly channels an Ascended Master called 'Tushwa' who had previously incarnated as one of the original Dalai Lamas. The symbol was thought to be a 55th dimension energy.

Over the next few days I undertook several meditations with the symbol, which I had carried around with me. I received information to the fact that the symbol, when incorporated with Reiki, could help reduce 'Karmic patterning' for those that seemed to be continuing to go through situations and experiences, even though the lesson had been learned. This would be especially good for souls attempting to progress spiritually but who are hampered by perceived karmic debt incurred in a less enlightened lifetime.

My own interpretation of the symbol was that the two facing shapes represented the 'as above... so below' concept. The fifth line is the link between the higher and lower selves, and the curly upward spiral indicates the alleviation from the physical plane, directed to the Divine.

At the beginning of May I was helping another Reiki practitioner with a treatment. As I was giving Reiki to the client's head I was involuntarily removed from my physical body. I had experienced similar situations but I would just observe the healing. This time I had a total out-of-body experience where I was taken completely away. Another entity entered my physical form and took over the healing. During the time that I was aware of my experience I was again shown the symbol of Grace and was given a hand-position and a name. I also became attuned to the symbol.

The hand position requires the practitioner to be at the head of the client. Both elbows are rested either side of the head and the fingers of both hands touch, creating a bridge effect over the client's eyes. The name given for this position was 'The Bridge of Souls'. When used - drawn in violet light and covered by the Power symbol - the practitioner needs to visualise water (alluding to the flow of the client's life) flowing under the bridge, down the body and out of the feet, never to return. The process is then sealed as normal with the Power symbol.

I regained awareness to find myself in a deep state of relaxation, performing the hand-position given. Looking up I was to see a very worried look on my friend's face. After the treatment I shared my experience with the other Reiki practitioner. I thought 'this is great!'. It was not to be the end of the story by a long way.

In late May I was beginning a teaching visit to Hong Kong and conducted an introduction night. At the end of the evening Jeff, an American living in Hong Kong, approached me. He said that he felt compelled to give me something, and thought that it could be important. We had a social drink together, when he declared that the something was an invocation. I nearly fell off the chair when he declared that the invocation was 'The Invocation of Grace'. The invocation read:

Let all beings, throughout all time, throughout all space, throughout all dimensions, and all planes of existence and non-existence, be forever liberated from all suffering, and fully experience the eternal joy of supreme liberation, now fully manifest!

Jeff explained that Buddhists believe that if only one soul can truly invoke this, it could relieve the karmic debt for all humanity. Reading through the invocation again, I realised that it did indeed cover everything, for everyone, at every time. I thanked him for the gift but wanted to assimilate what was happening before telling my part of the story.

Jeff further remarked that a three-day Buddhist ceremony of prayer, meditation and chanting was due to take place in a couple of weeks. He gave me the dates: those three days were when I had booked a Reiki Master class to be conducted at Mount Batur in Bali! By this time no further coincidence was going to shock me at all. I had been given a symbol, a hand position, a name and an invocation - all from different sources spanning thousands of miles - and now I had confirmation that I was to do something with it. I travelled from Hong Kong to Bali and a couple of days later met the candidates for the course. That evening we opened our circle on the beach and I informed those assembled about the story of Grace. Everybody was excited and felt, as I did, that we were coming together for something of import.

On 13th June 1995, under the brightest full moon I had ever seen, and in the shadow of Mount Batur's volcano, and the reflection of is lake, eleven new Reiki Masters were attuned. I was privileged to lead thirteen Masters in the Invocation of Grace that night. A feeling that something shifted that night was experienced. A couple of photographs of the moon were taken after the invocation, and in one a tremendous beam of light emanates towards us. Coincidence? I had given up on coincidence way before that time. The photograph remains a subject of awe to all those who experienced the immense power. I will always remember that special evening, connecting with many others in one great purpose, the relief of Karmic suffering for all.

The Grace symbol is taught to all Reiki Masters trained by myself. It will continue to be spread by those with a true commitment towards planetary enlightenment and the spiritual progression of mankind.

Go with Peace, Love, Light and Grace.

Simon Treselyan

Further information about the 'Grace' symbol (Taggart)

The way Treselyan's information is presented, it seems to suggest that karmic patterning is something that happens almost by unlucky chance, and a person just gets stuck in a groove and repeats a life lesson again and again for no good reason. I now understand that this is not the case: karmic patterning – for example going through a series of abusive relationships – is caused when a person does not learn the lesson. If a person does not learn the lesson and move on, then they are presented with another opportunity to learn the lesson and so on. So this symbol would be appropriate in any situation where a person is exhibiting repeated behaviour that is not good for them, e.g. overeating. The actual symbol that the 'Grace' symbol is based on is an old Taoist symbol used for karmic cleansing, apparently, and the actual symbol differs in a number of ways:

1   The symbol should be on its side (it has been channelled at the wrong angle!)
2   The lines should be traced out in a different order (see the diagrams below for both versions)
3   The final line should have five curves to it

The symbol should be visualised over a person's body while in the **seated** position. The symbol does not have a name - so you do not have to repeat any name as a mantra - and there is no associated hand position or special visualisation. This new information has come to me from a Chinese lady who grew up on a Buddhist monastery in Singapore, and learned this symbol during her training there.

Treselyan's Grace Symbol

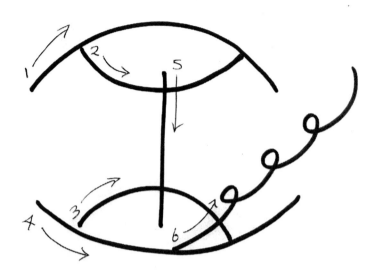

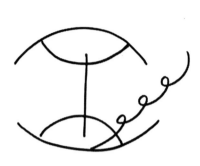

Taoist Grace Symbol

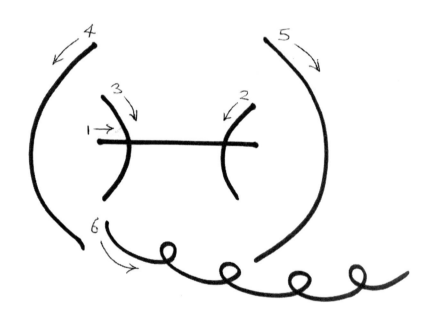

Meaning of the Pen Strokes

1	The human body
2	The soul
3	The lower chakras
4 & 5	The Auric field

This symbol is echoed in the final pen strokes of the symbol Hon Sha Ze Sho Nen

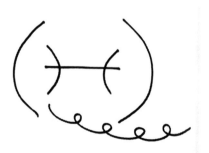

Symbol Meditations

The best way to get to grips with the new symbols and their energies - and you do need to become familiar with the energies if you are going to use them effectively - is to carry out energy meditations. This was Usui Sensei's original approach, and involved most of his students in carrying out various meditations or chanting kotodama over a long period of time to learn to experience earth ki, heavenly ki and oneness.

The Imperial Officers were taught symbols rather than meditations/kotodama but the symbols are still a way of depicting these energies. We do not know how the Imperial Officers used the symbols to experience their energies, or if indeed they used them in that way at all, but meditating on a symbol using the methods described below works well in practice.

Meditation #1

1. Sit with your eyes closed and your hands resting in your lap palms uppermost.
2. Draw out the symbol in your mind's eye, up in the air above you, and say its name to yourself three times, if it has a name.
3. Imagine cascades of energy flooding down onto you from the symbol.
4. Energy floods into your hands, into your head, into your torso, flowing over you, surrounding and engulfing you.

Be aware of any sensations in your body, any impressions, and qualities you are experiencing. Be aware of your emotions, your thoughts, and your state of mind, and where your attention dwells. Make notes afterwards on what you experienced.

Meditation #2

1. Sit with your eyes closed and your hands resting in your lap palms uppermost.
2. Draw out the symbol in your mind's eye, up in the air above you, and say its name three times if it has a name.
3. As you inhale, draw energy down from the symbol, into your crown.
4. Draw energy down the centre of your body to your Tanden *.
5. As you pause before exhaling, feel the energy get stronger in your Tanden.
6. As you breathe out, feel the energy spread through your body.

Make notes afterwards on what you experienced.

* The "Tanden" (Dantien in Chinese) is an energy centre that can be found approx. two finger-breadths below your tummy button and 1/3rd of the way into your body. In Oriental thought it is seen as your personal energy reserve, the centre of your creativity and intuition, the seat of your soul. It is used extensively in energy cultivation techniques like Tai Chi and Chi Kung, in Martial arts, in creative pursuits like calligraphy and flower arranging, and in the original form of Reiki!

Other Meditative Approaches

You can experiment with the Fire Dragon and the Spirit Column by visualising them in the air in front of you and then imagining that the symbol is moving towards you and merging with your body. What effects do you notice?

With all these techniques, you tend to notice more with time. As you repeat the exercises, the 'signature' of the energy seems to become more consistent and definite.

Students' Experiences

In this section you can read the experiences of some of our 'home study course' students in different parts of the world, talking about their work with some of the symbols found on this course. Maybe your experiences will echo theirs, maybe your experiences will be quite different.

"With TDKM I mentally experienced a 'stormforce' energy with torrential rain, thunder, lightning and the UDKM produced a huge sunrise and a feeling of nurturance and oneness. I felt a 'jolt' with the Fire Dragon when it entered my body which changed to a warm fizz all over. With the Mental Spiral I could actually feel the shape over my head like a hat and felt heat all over and a strong connection with the Solar Plexus. SKSK is much more gentle - like a cuddle
I find these two energies are more site specific while DKM's are all over, in and out and all around."

"I must say that I find the Tibetan DKM 'more colourful'. Each time I meditate on it I visualise this colourful fast tumbling, rolling cloud raining energy down on me. At first I feel it in my head and chest and then this feeling of weightlessness comes and I am this ball floating in space? I must admit that the first few times were pretty uneventful but recently, the above is what I feel and visualise. I find it quite easy to merge with this energy as well. The Usui DKM, on the other hand, is more difficult for me. I just don't seem to feel much with it. What does come to mind, though, is a ball of energy above me but the energy seems to stay there and I can't seem to bring it down."

And a few days later...

"Yahoo!!!! It happened. I try to do my meditating/practising (following your instructions in the Instruction Manual) first thing in the morning before I even get out of bed. This seems to work the best for me as once I get up, the time just races by and other things get in the way. Anyway, this morning I felt the Usui DKM energy and it was great. I finally asked my guides to help me out and after a few moments, it came. At first 'my head' filled with white/golden light and then a feeling of deep tranquillity came over me and I felt as if I were levitating. I felt a great love - very emotional and very beautiful. This came after 6 days of meditating on it - doing as you suggested (joshin kokkyu ho) - which I did this morning as well. I was getting so frustrated with it all but I persevered and I'm glad I did. I think I was trying too hard, not relaxing and staying in my head rather than merging with the energy. Leaving it up to my Guides to help out took the pressure off me and it just happened. I'm so happy - I thought I was going to be stuck in the Symbols section forever, ha, ha."

"My daily meditations: As I told you in my email, these were rather longer than 5 minutes on each master symbol energy to begin with. By the third day I began to use the intention that they would last for 5 minutes each just before I drew the symbols for each (as my 'sense of timing' had completely gone while doing them). By the end of the week they had settled into 5 minutes nicely :o)

"I have also found over the ten days that each energy has become more intense, and is now 'there' when I begin, instead of feeling it is 'building up' during each meditation. I've also found over the last two days that the energy is flowing into me before I have completed drawing the symbol above me :o), something I feel the frequency scale meditations have 'prompted' as my intention seems to be pre-empting the completion of the symbol? :o)

"Comparing the energies of the master symbols with CKR and SHK, I've found them to be of a much higher, 'lighter' vibration, yet with far more 'depth' and 'intensity' than CKR or SHK, and felt them to be on a 'different' level of healing energy, with most of the 'experiences' being felt within my aura levels. I also felt a difference between the Tibetan DKM and the Usui DKM, feeling the Usui DKM to be an even higher vibration. I've found it difficult to put down into words what I've experienced during my meditations on the Master symbols, because I'm finding there 'effect' almost by-passes my conscious mind, so please excuse my choice of words, and possible incoherence in my feedback.

"With the Tibetan DKM I feel a sense of peace, an upward lifting of my whole self, beyond my 'self', as if a great weight has been lifted from me. I feel as if I'm endlessly expanding out and I am far more aware of my energy body than anything else 'of myself'. I 'see' the colours emerald and gold (mostly gold). I find the energy very 'fine', 'subtle' yet intense all at the same time, and very 'comfortable/natural' :o).

"With the Usui DKM I find that the above experience steps up even further to a sense of total stillness. Time doesn't seem to exist and I am focussed only in now. I see the colours of white predominantly, with violet and indigo almost 'passing through'. There's an almost none discernible vibration with the Usui DKM as it feels just 'is' and 'now'. And I can only describe it as feeling as though I had truly 'tapped' into and 'become' the vibration of the source! Everything feels 'new' afterwards, as though it's 'a new day beginning', and I feel renewed and 'clearer', everything seems clearer.

"The Fire dragon symbol: I found this excellent to use after my master symbols because it felt as though the 'extremes' of the activity in my crown chakra were brought into my chakra system in full. I felt that my crown chakra was extremely active after the meditations, leaving me feeling a bit 'top heavy' and light headed energy-wise, yet after using this symbol it felt that my chakra system was more evenly balanced, my crown 'calmed down'. One thing I found very interesting too, was that as I visualised and allowed the symbol to 'sink into me' it took on the chakra colours in a wonderful rainbow array :o) and I felt a pulsing as it reached me.

"The Mental spiral and Heart chakra symbols: The mental spiral had me focussed totally on my thoughts and I have been getting flashes of memories that I hadn't consciously thought of in years. I felt the energy completely around my head and my third eye and crown chakra's, and I felt a slight coolness within the energy. The heart chakra symbol focussed completely on my heart area [as I would expect :o) !]. I felt an inner warmth and had the impression that I should breath through my heart chakra while meditating on this symbol, which I did, and found the 'feelings' intensified. I was 'seeing' washes of pinks and greens (also as I would expect, so I can't really say if these were 'my' input or from the energy!) flowing through the area. I also felt the energy pulsating gently. I felt that these energies were more intense than SHK, as if SHK was a combination of them, but that it had 'less intensity' through the combination as it was more in between the two. They were not physical feeling energies like CKR, and they didn't feel as high in vibration as the DKMs."

"Can tell you a bit about my work with the two DKM - with Usui DKM I feel as if I have lost all boundaries, as if I am pure energy, as if I have been lifted up to become one with the source and all things - it's very humbling.

"The Tibetan DKM I struggle with in that I feel as if I'm teetering on the edge of the same feeling that I get from Usui's DKM but there's something missing to make the connection complete. Like the lift has got stuck two floors short of the top. (sorry not good with descriptions)

" I used the Usui DKM to empower a hospital room yesterday - I can honestly say I've never experienced such power not coming just from my hands but my whole of the front of my body felt as if it was emanating light. I felt as if I was beginning to float off the floor. I could see the energy swirling round the room and us like a huge whirlpool of pure white light! I'd started with my hands held low at my side, but was drawn to bring them upwards and as I did so the energy rose from the floor to the ceiling, when the room was full I offered any excess for the highest good of anyone else in need at that time - not quite sure what to do in that situation."

The Reiki Kotodama

 Master Course Audio CD Number 1 - track #5

Background info

So, what are Kotodama? Well, they are phrases, vowel sounds, that play a important part in different aspects of Japanese life. Kotodama are found in these areas:

- Shintoism   as invocations
- Buddhism   as invocations and mantras in some aspects of Buddhism
- Martial Arts   as a way of focusing Ki

Kotodama are very old. The word means 'word spirit' or 'the soul of language'. Kotodama come from Shinto, the indigenous animist religion of Japan, though Japanese mystical (Mikkyo) Buddhism does have an equivalent practice where the sounds are referred to as "jumon".

When Buddhism arrived in Japan it incorporated a lot of Shinto practices in order to make itself acceptable to the local populace, and there is quite a lot of overlap between Shinto and Japanese Buddhism in terms of philosophy and practices. Interestingly, within mystical Buddhism, kotodama practice has been elaborated and mantras are used in conjunction with visual images (yantras) and special hand gestures (mudras) for a whole range of purposes. Perhaps we can see these practices echoed to an extent in the use of the Reiki symbols, which are based on the use of a repeated phrase and the visualisation of an image, though any use of mudras has not come through Dr Hayashi/Mrs Takata to the West, or indeed through any other source as far as I can see.

In any case, kotodama are based on the ancient idea of the sacred power of speech, and are used to both:

- Approach the divine
- Produce changes within the physical world

The idea is that the intonation of special sounds can bring about a mystical or spiritual state or achieve a particular outcome in the physical world. This is not a peculiarly Japanese notion, and the use of chanting and the idea of sacred sounds turns up in many cultures. A few examples could be the Kabbalah, Western Witchcraft, Transcendental Meditation, Nichiren Buddhism, and Tibetan Buddhism. Within Japan there are historical accounts of kotodama being used to stop armies in their tracks, to kill and to heal, and to control the weather.

It is said that at the birth of the physical and the spiritual world, there was the kotodama suuu, the core of existence, the very beginning of all things. This developed into U, and U split into two opposing forces: A and O. The kotodama represent the forces of the universe, and there is a collection of 75 kotodama that turns up in many aspects of Japanese life. They appear within Shinto and Buddhism as mantras for meditation, within Martial arts like Aikido, and within Reiki.

There is barely a handful of kotodama Masters in the whole of Japan now, and they take us back to the earliest of Japanese spiritual traditions, almost lost in the mists of time. Japanese people of earlier times believed that words had mystical power and that the fact of saying something could make it so since each syllable or kotodama could be thought of as divine aspects of creation. Modern Japanese people do not understand the kotodama, and they do not believe in them. They are seen as ancient Shinto practices. One example of their use, though, is by pearl divers: the girls who would undertake the dives would use the kotodama 'suuu' to still the waters before they dived in.

Some of the "New Religions" in Japan from the Meiji era to the present have diagrams that show how each sound in the Japanese language creates and sustains the universe. The founder of Aikido - Morihei Ueshiba - taught kotodama inspired by the new religion Omoto-kyo that was established by Usui and Ueshiba's contemporary, Onisaburo Deguchi, who was said to be a leading Kotodama Master at that time. The 'doka' poetry of Ueshiba was used in a similar way that Usui used Gyosei poetry...as teaching tools to help students capture the spirit of their teachings. Interestingly, the Waka poetry taught by Usui actually contains kotodama within it.

Kotodama were the way that Usui taught his students to connect with the different energies. They predate the use of symbols within Reiki. The Reiki symbols were only introduced into Reiki by Usui to help a few of his students - the three Naval officers - who were very much focused on treating others rather than working on the self, and who simply did not have the time to get to grips with the energies in the way that had Usui Sensei had used with his other students. The symbols were introduced as tools that you could use quickly to depict the energies in a treatment context. The intention was that in time you could leave the symbols behind and then work directly with the energies that they represented. Usui only taught the symbols to a few people it seems, including Dr Hayashi who, as we know, went on to make them an essential part of his practice.

Within Reiki, the kotodama represent the energies that we in the West use symbols to represent, but the kotodama are the original method, Usui's preferred method.

Why the Kotodama were taught

We now know that Mikao Usui's system was not about treating other people: it was all about working on the self. The system was about self-healing and spiritual development, and the treating of others was not emphasised or focused upon.

So when Usui Sensei introduced his students to three kotodama at Second Degree level, and these kotodama tie in with the three Reiki symbols taught at Second

Degree, he taught the kotodama because his students needed to get to grips with their energies to further their self-healing and spiritual development. Though the energies are useful when treating others, they were not introduced because of their relevance to treating others: they were there for the student's benefit.

The three kotodama taught at Second Degree level represented:

1. The energy of earth ki
2. The energy of heavenly ki
3. A state of oneness

Earth ki and heavenly ki are two fundamental energies that are worked with by practitioners of tai chi and qigong, and also turn up in Taoist and Shinto writings, so it is not surprising that these two energies feature in Mikao Usui's system. The third kotodama represents a state of oneness, and one of the goals of Usui Sensei's spiritual system was to achieve a state of oneness, which is seen from a Buddhist point of view as an experience of reality. A fourth kotodama was introduced to students at Master level, and you can read of its connotations in the Usui DKM section of this manual.

The Reiki kotodama have four names: Focus, Harmony, Connection and Empowerment.

- The focus kotodama represents earth ki and is represented by CKR in the Western system
- The harmony kotodama represents heavenly ki and is represented by SHK
- The connection kotodama represents a state of oneness and is represented by HSZSN
- The empowerment kotodama equates with the energy of the Usui DKM

Kotodama Pronunciation

The basic sounds are:

A   aaah
O   as in rose
U   as in true
E   as in grey
I   eee

Kotodama Name	Corresponding Reiki Symbol	The sound	Pronunciation Guide
Focus	CKR	ho ku ei	hoe koo ey eeee Ho rhymes with so, dough, go Ku rhymes with too, loo, moo
Harmony	SHK	ei ei ki	ey eeee ey eeee keee Ki rhymes with see, tree
Connection	HSZSN	ho a ze ho ne	hoe aaah zay hoe neigh Ho rhymes with so, dough, go Ze and Ne rhyme with day, say, play, may
Empowerment	Usui DKM	a i ko yo	aaah eeee coe yo Ko rhymes with so, dough, go Yo rhymes with so, dough, go

Kotodama Meditations

Here is a way of experiencing the energies of the Reiki kotodama:

1. Make yourself comfortable on a chair, with your hands resting on your lap or in the 'Gassho' position.
2. Focus your attention on your Tanden, two fingerbreadths below your tummy button and 1/3 of the way into your body.
3. Take a few deep breaths and feel yourself becoming peaceful and relaxed; clear your mind.
4. Chant the kotodama on each out-breath, using a deep, resonant voice.
5. Vibrate the kotodama from your Tanden, resonate the sound through your whole body; become the sound.
6. Do this for a few minutes, and when you have finished chanting, just be still and experience the quality of the energy, the ripples that continue, for a while.
7. Stay in that state for as long as feels appropriate.

If you wish to get to grips with the energies in the way that Usui taught, you will do this regularly to fully 'become' each energy. Usui Sensei would have had his students work with each kotodama for 6-9 months before moving on.

Comparing Kotodama and Symbol energies

The energies of the kotodama and the energy of the Reiki symbols are experienced differently by most people. It would be a good idea if you spent some time getting to grips with the differences between the two, and coming to your own conclusions about what the differences - if any - are. Here is a way of experiencing the energies of the symbols on your own, and should be done for 3-5 minutes for each symbol:

1. Sit comfortably with your eyes closed, with your hands resting in your lap and your palms facing upwards.
2. Visualise, say, **CKR** up in the air above you and say the name three times to empower the symbol.
3. Imagine cascades of energy flooding down onto you from the symbol. The energy radiates onto your face, your torso and into your hands, flooding through your whole body.

Here is an alternative method:

1. Sit comfortably with your eyes closed, with your hands resting in your lap and your palms facing upwards.
2. Visualise, say, **SHK** up in the air above you and say the name three times to empower the symbol.
3. As you breathe in, draw energy down from the symbol. The energy passes through your crown, down the centre of your body to your Tanden.
4. As you pause before exhaling, feel the energy getting stronger in your Tanden.
5. As you exhale, flood the energy throughout your body.

Once you have experienced the energy of CKR or SHK for a while, move on straight away to carry out a kotodama meditation, and thus compare the energy of the symbol with the energy of the corresponding kotodama.

So, draw down energy from CKR above you for a while, and then move on to chanting the focus kotodama. What difference is there in the energy?

Do the same with SHK /harmony and HSZSN /connection.

Come to your own conclusions about any differences between the energies.

Kotodama and Treatments

The Kotodama can be used as an alternative to the Reiki symbols when giving a treatment. So instead of using energy from CKR, for example, you could repeat the 'focus' Kotodama three times - or endlessly - to represent the energy. Use the 'harmony' Kotodama to represent the energy of SHK. One energy (or kotodama) would be used at any one time. You do not mix the energies in Usui's original form of Reiki, and this ties in with the way that I have been teaching the use of the Reiki symbols.

Experiment using the Focus and/or Harmony kotodama instead of the Reiki symbols when you treat, ideally introducing a kotodama when you feel strongly drawn to it – working intuitively – and see what response you get from the recipient. If they have received Reiki treatments from you in the past then maybe they will report some different experiences now that you are using the kotodama rather than symbols.

You might want to chant the connection kotodama silently to yourself for a little while at the start of a treatment by way of becoming one with the recipient.

Remember that the focus kotodama represents earth ki, the harmony kotodama represents heavenly ki, and the connection kotodama elicits a sense or state of oneness in the practitioner.

Kotodama and Distant Healing

This is a very simple method. Focus your attention on the recipient, chant the connection kotodama to yourself silently (or out loud if you like) and merge with the recipient; let the energy flow.

Kotodama and Crystals

The Japanese are not into crystals in a big way, but they turn up in Buddhist and Shinto practices. This technique uses three crystals; each one is charged with one of the second-degree energies, using the second-degree kotodama. The crystals are as follows:

1. Clear Quartz, charged using the 'connection' kotodama and placed on the 3rd eye.
2. Citrine, charged using the 'focus' kotodama and placed on the throat.
3. Jade - preferably unpolished - charged using the 'harmony' kotodama and placed on the heart.

These would be left in place during the treatment, and are said to produce a deep trance state. They can be charged by holding them, chanting the kotodama three times, and letting the energy flow. These three Chakras seem to hold some special significance within Buddhist meditation, as far as I understand it.

Using the Kotodama on your self

The kotodama meditations described above are a potent self-healing practice. Spend some time regularly chanting each kotodama and then being still, to experience the energy, the ripples, that follow. If you trained with Mikao Usui you would have chanted the focus kotodama for 6-9 months to fully assimilate that energy, to become that energy, before moving on to spend a similar period of time working with the harmony kotodama.

A few of Usui Sensei's students moved on to work long-term with the connection kotodama, to fully experience a state of oneness, one of the goals of the original system.

Kotodama and Chakras

Although there is no evidence that this was performed by Usui Sensei's students or taught by Usui, you might want to experiment by chanting the kotodama "in" your chakras, resonating the sound (in your imagination) "from" your root Chakra for a while, then from you sacral Chakra etc. Spend a few minutes chanting the kotodama from each Chakra from the root to the crown.

Start using the focus kotodama; maybe do that for a week or so.

Then use the harmony kotodama for a week or so.

Notice what happens as you do this, and the ongoing effects.

In the "Intuition" section you will learn to determine which aspect of a Chakra may need to be dwelt upon in order to achieve balance.

Students' Experiences

In this section you can read the experiences of some of our 'home study course' students in different parts of the world, talking about their work with the kotodama. Maybe your experiences will echo theirs, maybe your experiences will be quite different.

"I felt the energy through the kotodama very strongly, especially immediately after the chanting, when the vibration of the sound appeared to be in the whole of my body, almost as if I became the sound, and it appeared to be an unconscious use - I thought this is what you mean by 'getting your head out of the way'. Energies of each kotodama reflected the energies I was previously getting from the symbols. During the chanting, my own body took on the vibrations so much so that I could actually feel a swaying. Chanting also seems to strengthen the feelings and create further resonances. During the Empowerment kotodama chant the syllables merged, and the sound seemed as if it was coming from someone else! I felt that Focus was the heaviest, while Harmony is lighter and of a different vibration. Connection, on the other

hand felt like I was in a time machine and I sensed a 'travelling' in my 3rd eye, rather than in my body or hands. Empowerment is all over.

"Practised 2 Reiki treatments using the kotodama. Treatment one was with 2nd degree practitioner who felt the differences in the vibrations almost as soon as they changed. She reported getting a lot of colours and geometric patterns - differing from each kotodama. I particularly felt more attached to Reiki than ever before, and more able to channel the energy.

"Treatment 2 was with a Master who felt the Kotodama enter her body and travel from the crown to the feet. Could it be that she received any attunement here? She felt the vibrations within her chakras. She said that this was a different treatment to any she has had before. She said she felt the presence of many 'guides' and that a lot seemed to be going on at an etheric level. Actually after the chanting it seemed to me that the whole space of the room was vibrating, that it was waiting in a stillness - does that sound strange to you? I felt that I was connecting to something very powerful.

"The Connection kotodama proved to be very exciting, with me experiencing being in a sort of tunnel and whooshing through time and space. I was there with the person receiving the distant healing. I felt as if I could be anywhere at anytime that I chose."

"Focus kotodama - this makes me feel very heavily relaxed and very warm. My focus is completely on my physical body. I see the colours of reds, browns and greens. I feel myself being drawn down/sinking, and feel very grounded, and I can smell soil/earthy aroma's, and sometimes I almost feel as if I am surrounded by earth.

"Harmony kotodama - this makes me feel very light, relaxed, and cool. I find my focus on my mental level mostly, and just outside of my physical body into the 'lower' levels of my aura. The colour I see is light greens. I feel as if I'm being lifted up on air, and had the sensation of floating.
Connection kotodama - this makes me feel 'connected', a part of everything around me. I feel that I can be with whoever I think about, or wherever I think about without any difficulty. If I focus on someone I feel myself being drawn to them, then feel as though I'm with them, and 'connected' to them.

"Empowerment kotodama - this takes me right away from any physical/emotional/mental focus completely, I just feel still, and absorbed completely in the now, and extremely light, akin to being completely out of my body. When I 'connect' I feel as if I whoosh upwards. Everything is white, like a blank canvas in a way, and just 'is'. The vibration feels very high, and after I always feel refreshed, everything seems clearer and brighter, like just waking at the start of a bright new day :o) and I feel quite encumbered having to move my body around then!

"In comparing the energy of the symbol and kotodama - I've found that each symbol and it's corresponding kotodama are very similar, both in vibration and essence, but...the huge difference I have noticed is the way that I feel about connecting with them and their 'strength'/depth. When I use the kotodama I find the energy much more intense, and it seems to be of a much deeper 'essence' (oh here I go, can't find the right words again, sorry). It's also 'there' quicker, the flow is more immediate, either in myself experiencing it for a meditation, or for use in a healing. I also feel connected to the energy more strongly, as if from inside with the kotodama, rather than from outside with the symbol. For me, I feel that using the kotodama is 'setting up' the energy I'm choosing from within me, [as though I'm setting up my vibration to match the kotodama's energy while chanting?!?], rather than connecting to the energy that is flowing from the symbol outside of me and drawing that energy down into me..... Oh I do hope that makes sense :o).... and I've always found sound to be 'mood'/emotion stimulation, so I feel that chanting the kotodama is a far more 'natural' connection method to me to use."

Using kotodama on others...

"Both of my friends felt the treatment was more intense than ones they have had from me before (partly my reason for 'using' them, as they have received treatments before, and have both felt different experiences). While using the focus kotodama, one felt extremely sleepy, and spent most of the time yawning, they both felt extremely relaxed, heavy and warm. One saw no colours at all, but the other constantly saw browns and deep reds, they also both felt very physically focussed and grounded. One felt that my hands were moving back and forth in small movements all the time (yet they were actually still), both felt heat from my hands. While using the harmony kotodama, both felt cooler, one saw lots of pink, and both felt the 'sensations' in another part of their bodies. While at the heart chakra area on one, the sensation of warmth was felt in the stomach area (this is where she has physical symptoms if she is emotionally upset). One felt nothing while I had my hands around their solar plexus, but as soon as I moved them away, they felt a 'chill' (which they explained as feeling like the 'chill' you feel on your face after you have used a menthol steam inhalation over a bowl.)

"For my own part, both of the treatments felt much more intense than when using the symbols, and I found that I remained in my intuited hand positions for a long time, and used less hand positions than would be considered 'normal', the energy was flowing out in a larger 'radius' in some places (which I felt was because there was no 'focus area' that the energy was specifically needed in), but also I had several hand positions that were close together and felt that the healing was more 'in depth' in those areas. Also, I found that both my friends were feeling things in areas away from where my hands were when I was using the harmony kotodama. I treated one person hands on, yet the other I felt I needed to treat hands off, so did so. When using the focus kotodama I was very hot, and with the person I was treating hands on, I felt that I had to keep checking that I wasn't pressing down on them, as I felt my hands were very heavy and as if I was leaning forward onto them. In one hand position on one of them I felt them 'drawing' so much energy that my hands ached. My one friend needed more physical healing, and the other needed more emotional healing, and I found that my feelings of which kotodama to use coincided with what I knew of their needs. In fact I often found that the energy they needed was flowing before I actually used any kotodama, so I used the kotodama for that energy to strengthen what they were receiving.

"As it happened, I had a friend who came down with a very nasty cold, with a sinus and chest infection, the day before I had arranged to do a distant healing on her (which I didn't find out until afterwards). We both sat at the arranged time, and I began the healing with the connection kotodama. I had no problem with actually 'being' with her for the healing, I felt as if I was actually standing behind her in her chair. In fact it turned into a half hour treatment with intuitive hand positions!! I treated her crown, temples, ears/side of head, forehead, throat, sides of her neck and her chest area. At all positions I felt I was 'sending' Earth ki energy, so I used the focus kotodama. At the end I smoothed her aura, and handed her a red butterfly?!? I spoke to her a few minutes later over the internet. She had felt when I had began, and when I finished, (and was surprised about how long it had lasted, I had originally asked her to sit for about 20 minutes to make sure I had finished!?!).. and as she opened her eyes afterwards, she saw a robin sitting on her windowsill!!! She told me how awful she had felt before I began, and that she had felt as if I was drawing 'stuff' out of her the whole time. She could tell where I was 'working' at each position. She felt that her chest and sinus's were totally clear afterwards. I also sent her distant healing daily for the rest of the week, which I 'set up' for her to collect in the evening (she is in America, so the time difference meant that we couldn't 'get together' at the same time again because of her working hours). She suffered no more sinus or chest problems, and the rest of her cold lasted for about three days. I have also been sending healing to a friend each night who has been suffering from bad night's of sleep (or should I say lack of sleep). Each night I have sent her 10 minutes of Reiki distantly, to 'collect' when she goes to bed. She has been sleeping soundly all week!!

"I have always found that I am able to 'be' with someone when I'm sending them distant healing, using the connection kotodama though, I feel even more 'there' and find that I don't need to focus on 'staying there' the way I sometimes needed to before, so I can concentrate my attention on the healing fully."

"Since I have been chanting the kotodama aloud and silently there is not a single area of my life that has not been affected. Even the awareness of them produces a shift in my energy, thinking and my actions. The symbols seem a bit cumbersome at times and not as effective or "user friendly" as the kotodama. Especially during treatments.

"I find the Focus energy to be hot and very noticeable during treatment of clients. The energy moving through my body is very noticeable. For example: there have been times when my spine would straighten. It is very easy to discern. The Harmony feels more gentle, like infusion and I liken it to cooler feeling, blue. Invoking the Harmony kotodama makes me very aware of my heart and at times it feels as if I am collapsing within myself, my heart. It is very beautiful to treat with this energy. The Connection kotodama totally amazed me. I had not experienced such a blending with my clients before. It is easier for me to scan than use Reiji ho but the Connection helps. I am surprised on how subtle it feels. My experience with the Empowerment kotodama is blissful at times. My body feels like moving, alive energy. And during treatment the Reiki seems to move somehow deeper into the body. My hands feel as if they are in the client's body at times. At times I am aware of white light.

"My friend and peer, Diane came for treatment. She has a thyroid disorder and her doctors suggested surgery. Diane knows that there is another way to approach the situation......After seeing another physician, it was thought that stress is a factor. So Diane asked for healing on a mental and spiritual level. With the Connection kotodama my focus on the treatment remained constant. With both the Harmony and Empowerment I was able to hear where to go next. The energy felt of a finer vibration, as if the energy was received at a cellular level, very deep inside.

"I am becoming accustomed to blending and becoming one with the recipient, but not following them in their imbalances. The feeling is a comforting and pleasant one. And because no thought is required, I feel confident."

Freestyle Practice

Introduction

This section is all about freeing up our practice of Reiki. I want to explore some of the things that are possible with Reiki when you suspend your disbelief and simply try things out. Our Reiki practice is limited only by our beliefs and assumptions: if we believe that something is not possible then we are shooting ourselves in the foot before we even begin, and we probably will not even try. So we are going to be exploring the power of our intent, and discovering how intuitive we already are.

But what I want to do first in this section, to put things in context, is to review and summarise the approaches to giving Reiki treatments and Self-treating that will have been covered on my First and Second Degree courses; then we can move on to describe what I see as the ideal when working on the self and on others, and explore some of the possibilities that are available to us when we work with Reiki, in terms of intent and intuition.

Treating at Reiki1 & Reiki2 Levels

First Degree

On my Reiki First Degree courses, students are taught to use some standard hand positions, not set in stone, and they know that they will move beyond those standard hand positions in time. They are taught scanning, which shows them where they are going to be spending longer when they treat, and scanning may suggest some alternative or additional hand positions. They are told that they may start to receive some intuitive impressions, for example being strongly drawn to a particular area, and that they should just go with such impressions and treat the areas they are drawn to, without analysing or trying to rationalise the impressions they receive.

The state of mind that I encourage them to have as they treat is one of having disappeared into the energy and merged with it, so they 'become one' with the energy. No thoughts, no expectations, just merging with the energy and allowing it to happen. Sometimes students may notice that by imagining that they are drawing energy down from above, they notice more happening in their hands as the treat.

The energy flows through the student at whatever frequency is appropriate for the recipient at any particular moment. Thus the energy deals with either the physical or the mental/emotional aspects of anyone treated, or there may be effects on a soul or spiritual level. Reiki will come through in a way that suits the recipient.

Reiki Second Degree

The Second Degree empowerments (or attunements for that matter) seem to allow practitioners to channel greater amounts of energy when compared to First Degree, though this is partly just because they have received another connection, rather than anything special about the empowerments at this level. In Usui Sensei's system it was intended that you receive empowerments again and again throughout your training at all levels, and this could be seen as allowing you - little by little - to hold and transmit more and more energy, or it could be seen as a way of repeatedly 'clearing' your energy system; the effects of this build up progressively over time.

I need to make it clear that Reiju empowerments, used as a way as 'connecting' a student to Reiki, are just as effective as Western attunements and in my opinion have several advantages. Receiving Western attunements repeatedly would be a beneficial practice, too, because of the effect of - little by little - allowing the student to hold and transmit more energy, and I notice that William Rand (a well known American Reiki teacher) recommends that his Master students get together to repeat attunements on each other. He recommends this not because attunements are in some way weak or ineffective, and need to be repeated; there are simply benefits that come through repeating them, just like Reiju empowerments.

In any case, quite often this 'increased energy flow' that can come after going on a Second Degree course is noticeable to the practitioner and the recipient, particularly if the recipient has been receiving some treatments from a First Degree practitioner and then goes on to receive a treatment from the same person, newly-attuned at Second Degree. They can compare, and often things seem stronger or deeper.

In Usui Sensei's system you were not 'attuned' to symbols, so when I use Reiju empowerments on my Reiki Second Degree courses the students are not attuned to any symbols. Although it has been a firm belief of Western style Reiki that the symbols will not work for you unless you have been specifically attuned to them, I can state quite categorically that this is not the case. Once you are connected to the energy then the symbols will work for you. They simply represent different aspects of what you already have within you.

Usui's Second Degree empowerments 'show' the two energies to you (earth ki and heavenly ki), or 'flag up' the energies to you, and to get the greatest benefit out of the system at this level then you need to work with the energies regularly to thoroughly 'assimilate' or 'become' them. A good way of doing this is to carry out the symbol meditations described in the Second Degree manual, and by using the symbol meditation on the Reiki2 audio CD. One of the empowerments 'shows' you the state of oneness (this is not an energy) and you can be come more familiar with this state through carrying out distant healing.

Second Degree practitioners can still carry out 'simple' Reiki treatments where they let the energy flow as it wishes, and the energy will still flow at whatever frequency is required. Because you have been introduced to the symbols does not mean that you are obliged to use those symbols all the time in practice when you treat.

This is an important point to make, I think, because some students are told that they have to use the symbols all the time once they have been through Second Degree.

Each symbol used in treatments generates energy at a certain frequency, and the frequencies that can be emphasised at Reiki Second Degree level are those of **ChoKuRei** or **SeiHeKi**, the low frequency 'physical healing' energy and the higher frequency 'mental/emotional balancing' energy. Using a symbol boosts the flow of energy and focuses the energy on physical healing or mental/emotional balancing. Usui Sensei's students saw these energies as those of earth ki and heavenly ki.

Hon Sha Ze Sho Nen is not a symbol that produces energy of a particular frequency: in the West it is often seen as a prayer asking for the energy to be connected in a particular way, and does not affect the frequency of the energy being channelled or the amount of energy that is being channelled. In Original Reiki it represents and elicits a state of Oneness, allowing you to transcend time and space.

On the Second Degree course we touch on some ways of boosting the flow of energy, which can be used occasionally if we find a part of the body is drawing a lot of energy, and we can boost the flow of energy further if we wish.

Second Degree introduces the student to intent and intuition. The 'many hands' method shows that the energy will focus itself wherever the practitioner focuses their intention, or attention, with the 'hands' visualisation being a convenient way of focusing attention on a particular area of the body. The 'sending Reiki with the eyes' again demonstrates that whether we are treating or sending distant Reiki, the energy focuses itself where we are focusing our attention, with various rituals and visualisations merely serving as a focus or a 'hook' to direct our attention.

The Reiji ho method introduced at Second Degree allows the student to move away from the standard hand positions taught at First Degree to go more 'freestyle', where they allow the energy to guide their hands to the right places to treat. The key to success with Reiji ho is to not try, to not think, not analyse, not notice what is going on in the hands, but to simply merge with the energy, bliss out on the energy, and let the movements happen. In effect, you are in a mindful state. The more practice we have at getting our conscious mind out of the way and cultivating that lovely empty, merged state, the easier Reiji ho becomes. In fact that state of mind was introduced at first-degree level, and is also used when sending distant healing.

On Second Degree it is emphasised to the student that the ideal when using Reiki is to get your head out of the way and allow the energy to guide you, or to allow your intuition to guide you, both in terms of where you put your hands and in terms of what aspect of the energy – which symbol, if any – you use.

So that is where we should have come to so far, before commencing the Master/Teacher course, and what I would like to do now is to delve further into the subject of intent and intuition.

The Use of Intent

 Master Course Audio CD Number 1 - track #6

Intent is a lot more important than we realise. Reiki is very simple: it follows our thoughts, it follows our focus. This section considers the ways that we are already using our intent when working with Reiki, and shows some of the things that are possible. We will explore:

1. Radiating Reiki
2. Distant Healing and Intent
3. Remote Treatments
4. Focusing the Energy on yourself using Intent
5. Controlling the nature of the Energy using Intent

Intent during Reiki Treatments

You will be familiar with the 'many hands' technique (taught on the Reiki2 course) where you can intensify the Reiki effect by imagining a couple of extra sets of arms on either side of your body, and feel the energy flowing through your imaginary arms and hands as well as the real ones. Some people who have used this technique have found that they can feel heat/energy flowing from the imaginary hands (for example into the back of their real hands), and some recipients have felt heat/energy entering their body from the place where the imaginary hands were. Some people can actually feel which imaginary hand was put into place in what order!

Actually, the visualisation of extra sets of arms and hands in not a necessary step. The important thing is that you are allowing your attention to rest or to dwell in a number of different areas at the same time. You could achieve the same results by imagining disembodied hands in different positions, or by imagining no hands at all, simply by focusing your attention in a number of areas at the same time. Since the energy follows your focus, if your attention is resting along the length of the entire leg then the energy will focus itself and flow there too, though of course where the energy goes is also controlled by the need of the recipient.

When treating the temples, we could imagine extra hands hovering over the front of the face and cupping round the back of the head, cocooning the head with energy. Again we do not necessarily have to visualise hands: we can allow our attention to envelop the head to the same effect. You do not even need to have your hands resting on the person's body for this to work: simply focus your attention on an area and the energy will flow there.

If you are treating the front of the body, maybe you could imagine an extra set of hands 'mirroring' the real set, so you treat both sides of the body at the same time.

Some people believe that you should treat both sides of a client, and this technique achieves that without the physical need to turn them over, always very disruptive for the recipient!

We can make the energy flow through the body to a particular area if we wish: we could treat the shoulders, for example, and intend that the energy should travel to a particular part of the body, for example the leg. It will do that: energy follows thought.

"Eye" and "Breath" Techniques

Many people are now experimenting with Koki Ho and Gyoshi Ho, the 'Gakkai techniques where you send Reiki using your eyes or your breath. They are effective. But when you are using the 'eye' technique, for example, I do not believe that the energy is flying out of your eyeballs like Clark Kent raising his eyes to send laser beams. I believe that you are simple *making* the energy go to the other person, and you are constructing a little visualisation in order to achieve that. Because you are imagining that the eyes are involved, then the energy is transmitted in a way that picks up on some of the connotations of looking or staring: the energy is sent/received in a piercing, intense, focused way. Energy sent using the breath seems to be received in a much more of a billowing or superficial way, picking up on the connotations of breathing onto someone.

These techniques are simply a practical example of intent. You can send Reiki out of the soles of your feet if you like, maybe to treat a dog that you are resting your feet on. I can't think of too many applications for this method!

"Radiating" Reiki

You can flood Reiki out of your entire body to someone else who is sitting across the room from you if you like. This method can be used to send Reiki to a client who is sitting telling you about their problems.

You can carry this out as an experiment with another Reiki person: the recipient sits with their eyes closed and thinks about a difficult or sad event in their lives, connecting with the thoughts and emotions that they would have felt at that time, making themselves feel thoroughly miserable. After a minute or so the 'sender' (sitting with their eyes closed and their hands in their lap) simply feels that they are connecting with the other person's thoughts and emotions. They intend that Reiki is radiating out of their body, flooding to the other person, surrounding and engulfing them.

Most recipients feel unable to continue focusing on the sad event in their life. Their reaction varies: some people forget what it was that they were focusing on, others find that the situation is resolved now, so they don't really feel bad about it any more, others find that the situation is being 'walled up' by a layer of white mist, so they cannot direct their attention on the past event any longer... and it no longer makes them sad.

All this can be done while you are just sitting there (and of course you can use this technique with your eyes open too).

Intent and Distant Healing

If you are thinking nice warm thoughts about someone, then *dzzzzt* ... you have just sent distant healing to that person, you have sent them Reiki because you were focusing your attention on them and Reiki follows what you are focusing on. This concept would obviously cause problems for people who believe that you should not send Reiki to people without getting their permission first. They would have to make sure that they only *thought* about a person if they obtained their permission first!

*This is why on my second degree courses I tell people that there is no problem in sending Reiki to people who have not requested it, so long as your intent is neutral: you cannot **not** send Reiki, because it is with you always, directing itself according to your focus.*

Distant Healing without symbols

Obviously the above example does not involve the use of the Reiki symbols, or the Reiki kotodama. They are not essential for distant Reiki to work, and neither are the detailed and complex rituals and set forms of words that some people are taught. If you want Reiki to go somewhere, then just make it go and it will be there as you intended. The symbol and the kotodama make you familiar with the process, help you to experience the right state of mind, but you can access that state of mind directly once you are familiar with it, through practice and repetition.

Try some experiments with another Reiki person: send distant healing using nothing but direct intent. You could arrange to do this with someone in a different town, or with a Reiki person who is sitting near you: sit with your hands in your lap, close your eyes (so you're not sending with your eyes!) and send the Reiki distantly to their head, or their heart, or their abdomen... and see what they notice. Did they feel Reiki where you sent it?

"Remote Treatments"

Since you can make a simple connection with another person at a distance using intent, and since you can direct the energy to various parts of their body using visualisation/intent, then why not try experimenting with doing a full treatment on someone at a distance.

This is not distant healing – where you are sending Reiki in a very general way - because you are actually directly connecting to, focusing on, and engaging with the other person for an extended period of time, say 40 minutes. You can sense their energy and direct the energy intuitively. Start with the shoulders, and follow a series of hand positions, finishing with the ankles maybe, just like a 'live' treatment, but directing the energy into different positions using visualisation/intent.

In the "Intuition" section of this manual you will discover how it is possible to combine remote treatments with remote intuitive working, directing the energy at a distance, and intuitively, into just the right combination of positions for them on that occasion.

The Self-Treatment Meditation

Moving now to self-treatments, the Usui Self-treatment meditation is another example of focusing the energy into different areas. You can visualise yourself treating a carbon copy of yourself, you can imagine yourself being treated by a carbon copy of yourself – or some disembodied hands – or you can allow your attention to dwell on the different areas of your head. In each case the energy will follow your focus and flow there.

Intent and Hands-On Self-Treatments

You are not restricted to focusing the energy only onto your head using intent: if you are doing a hands-on self-treatment, for example, and you cannot get your hands in a position so that they can rest on the part you want to treat, then just intend that your hands are resting on the chosen area, or imagine that the energy is flowing to that area.

Imagine that you are lying on your back on the bed. You want to treat your back. You could simply rest your hands on your abdomen and intend that the energy flow from your hands to the back. It will do that, and your back may heat up as if there were hot water bottles underneath you!

You can even 'cut out the middle man' and imagine that the energy is cascading into your crown, travelling through your body to the area of need. It will do that.

What you imagine is what will happen.

Focusing on Organs and Chakras

Now of course if you can focus the energy on various parts of your body using intent/visualisation then there is no reason why you can't be quite specific when doing this, for example by focusing the energy on various body organs or on particular chakras.

Within Taoism there is a practice referred to as "The Inner Smile" where you focus warm thoughts and compassionate feelings towards various internal organs, like your Liver, Spleen, Small Intestine, Lungs. If we did this as a Reiki person, the energy would follow our focus and direct itself on the organs that held our attention.

We can also focus Reiki on our chakras using intent. Visualise your root Chakra and imagine Reiki focusing there. Allow the energy to dwell there for a few minutes before moving on to the next Chakra. In the "Intuition" section of this manual you will discover a way to find out which Chakra requires extra attention.

Intent and the Nature of the Energy you Channel

We cannot only control where the energy goes, in others, and ourselves, but we can also control the nature of the energy itself if we wish.

You will be familiar with the technique where you visualise a big version of a symbol up in the air above you and draw down energy from that symbol to you, flooding the energy over you and through you for a while. There is a guided meditation on the Second Degree audio CD that talks you through such a symbol meditation. We do this to further our self-healing and spiritual development, and so that we become thoroughly familiar with the energies of these symbols. We can also draw down energy from a symbol above us as we treat.

You will have experienced the energies of Cho Ku Rei and Sei He Ki as quite distinct and characteristic.

You will also remember that one can view CKR as producing a low frequency energy that resonates at the frequency of the physical body, with SHK producing a higher frequency energy that resonates near the frequencies of our mental and emotional bodies.

"Frequency Setting"

 Master Course Audio CD Number 2 - track #3

On that basis, we could carry out an energy meditation where we simply intend that we are drawing down a low frequency energy suitable for dealing with the physical body, and imagine that energy building up and intensifying in our hands. After a while we could imagine that we are receiving a higher frequency energy that resonates at the level of thoughts and emotions, and imagine that this energy builds up and intensifies in our hands. We could imagine a 'frequency scale' with a little pointer that slides up and down from "physical" to "mental/emotional", and maybe slides even further up the scale to a level that ties in with the energy of the spirit or soul.

And if you can direct the nature of the energy in this way, after becoming thoroughly familiar with the two energies, then there is the potential there for you to direct the nature of the energy using intent as you treat if you like. You do not *have* to give up using the symbols - they are effective and useful – but there is the potential there for you to move beyond them to access the energies directly if you wish. There are no short cuts though: you can only move beyond the symbols to access their energies direct once you have spent a long time becoming thoroughly familiar with those energies, by meditating on them and by using them in practice when you treat.

This is simply a possibility that is available to you.

"Frequency exercise is very good and helps when trying to feel the difference between the energies. I found that my hands seemed to tingle higher each time."

"The Frequency scale: I loved this :o) By today I've found that I can 'turn it up and down' really well :o) As I begin to 'see' the pointer moving up or down the scale the energy instantly moves with it. As I've said above, I feel it has also affected my other meditations and using the symbols. I've always believed that intention has a great deal to do with sending healing, especially at a distance, and to me this is proof that my intention to change the energy vibration is all that is needed, my intention that the healing will reach the person is all that is needed, or maybe I should say is the 'most important requirement'. I can't draw any of the symbols, or even connect to Reiki without the intention that what I am 'doing' will happen, which to me strengthens the need for intent, and also shows the ultimate 'simplicity' of Reiki. By intending to 'send' or 'link' to SHK energy (for example), the use of the symbol is extra, as I have already begun to 'use' that level of energy by intending to. I can accept easily that if my intention is to strengthen the flow of energy that can happen too, within my own capabilities, eventually without the need for symbols, as my focus gets better with each use :o)"

The Use of Intuition

 Master Course Audio CD Number 1 - track #7

Extending your Intuition

You are already intuitive. You should have realised that now since you have been practising Reiji ho, where the energy guides your hands to the right places to treat. But this is not the only way in which you can work intuitively: you can access further insights about the energetic state of other people, and about yourself.

Basic Reiji Ho

 Master Course Audio CD Number 2 - track #4

The "Reiji ho" method with which you are familiar involves hovering your hands motionless over a person, allowing the energy to flow, feeling yourself disappearing into the energy and merging with it, and allowing your hands to drift with no expectations. The technique works best when you don't try, when you don't think, don't analyse, it works best when you get your head out of the equation, merge with the energy and let it happen.

With time it becomes easier and easier to click into that empty, merged state, and over time the hand movements become more definite, more deliberate, more consistent and less slow. It is a wonderful way to work because of the lovely merged state that you get yourself into in order to practise it, and intuitive treatments produce benefits for the recipient too because you are directing the energy into just the right combination of positions for them on that occasion... and on subsequent treatments your hand positions change as their energy needs change.

Selective Reiji Ho

When you practise Reiji ho you seem to be guided by the energy to a 'composite' picture of the recipient's energy needs and priorities on all levels, encompassing their physical, their mental/emotional and their spiritual needs too. But using intent you can carry out Reiji ho 'selectively' if you choose, so that you are guided to areas of physical need, or areas of mental/emotional need, or areas of spiritual need perhaps. This might be an interesting way to work for a while, so you can discover where such areas are located. It may give you some useful information.

As you carry out Reiji, the way to do this would be to have in your mind 'please let me be guided to areas of physical need' etc.

Imaginary Reiji Ho

When you carry out Reiji ho you are allowing intuitive knowledge – from your subconscious mind – to control your hand movements. You are moving your hands: your brain, your nerves, your muscles, in the same way that when people dowse with a pendulum, the pendulum moves because the dowser is jiggling it... but it is not the conscious mind that is controlling the movements.

So we have the subconscious providing us with guidance, and this guidance manifests itself as muscle movements. But that is not the only way that intuitive information can reach us.

You will be familiar with the 'extra set of hands' method, where you control where Reiki is going to focus itself based on where you are focusing your attention; as a convenient shortcut, you focus your attention on specific areas of the body by imagining that you have extra sets of hands, with energy or light flooding out of the imaginary hands into various treatment positions. The visualisation is just a convenient way of focusing your intent/attention.

Now consider what might happen if you were to hover imaginary hands over the person in your mind's eye... you should find that the imaginary hands will drift in your mind's eye to the areas of need, just like your real hands did. In fact, if you now try using Reiji ho with real hands, they are likely to drift into just the same positions that your imaginary hands did. The same intuitive information has manifested itself in two different ways: through muscle-movements and through an imagined visual image.

And of course you could play around with this and use the imaginary hands selectively, asking to be guided to areas of physical need, mental/emotional need etc.

And because this is in your imagination, if you like you can shrink your hands down to a smaller size, and zoom in like a telephoto lens to look in more detail at the exact areas of need, not just the general area.

Remote Intuitive Work

Intuition works whether the recipient of your attention is right in front of you or 1,000 miles away, so long as your attention is focused on them. So if you are talking on the telephone to someone, for example, you might bring up into your mind's eye and 3D image of them – which you could rotate if you liked – and see where your imaginary hands want to drift.

Distance is no barrier to working intuitively.

Remote Scanning

Because you are 'connected' to another person no matter what the distance, you could try doing scanning on someone when they are standing the other side of the room, moving your hands along the length of their body and feeling the sensations in your hands to detect 'hotspots' or fizzy areas or areas of need. In fact you can try this with your hands motionless, just intending that your hands are over particular areas and noting what sensations you receive.

Try scanning when the person is no longer present in the room - remote scanning - and you should find that this is just as effective. Give it a try. Either imagine your imaginary hands hovering and moving over their imaginary body, or use a 'prop' like a teddy bear or a doll, and scan the prop.

Given a choice I would tend to use Reiji Ho rather than scanning, but that's just my personal preference. Some people really get on well with scanning, though.

Intuition and Remote Treatments

So if we can intuit areas of need using our intuition/visualisation, and if we can direct the energy at a distance simply using our intent/visualisation, then we could carry out a whole Reiki treatment at a distance, intuiting the best hand positions and directing the energy into those areas using intent.

This is not the same as sending distant healing because you are sending the energy in a precise and focused fashion rather than in a general sense, and it would require quite a fair amount of concentration on your part for a fair chunk of time, but the possibility is there.

Enhancing Your Perception

You know more than you realise about the state of your energy system, and that of other people. You **know** what is going on with your Chakra system; you **know** what is going on with the Chakra system of other people. To access this intuitive information you need to focus your attention in a particular way, and be open to receive intuitive impressions. We can also use visual constructs in our mind's eye to access intuitive information, and we will deal with both of these areas below.

Directly Experiencing Someone's Chakras

Try this experiment with another person. They sit near you:

1. Close your eyes.
2. Remind yourself of your connection to the energy through your crown.

3. Imagine energy flooding down to you from above, through the centre of your body to your Tanden.
4. Feel/imagine the energy building up and becoming more intense in your Tanden.
5. Focus your attention on the other person.
6. Feel yourself merging with the other person, becoming one with them.
7. Consider their chakras; be aware of their chakras. Have no expectations of what you may experience.
8. How do they seem to you?
9. Is your attention pulled towards one or some of them?
10. Do they seem balanced, or do they seem not quite right somehow; in what way? Can you see them? Can you feel them? What impressions you have about their state?
11. Do this for maybe 5 minutes and then withdraw your attention back to you; withdraw the energy back to you.

You may be surprised to find that you have perceived the Chakras as having quite distinct characteristics compared to each other, and you may have a strong feeling about which Chakras seem fine, which Chakras require some attention, and which ones need boosting rather than restraining. You may also notice that in some people the Chakras will not seem all nice and even and the same size, yet your impression is that this is the correct 'presentation' for them, that it is ok for a particular Chakra to be bigger or more prominent. So we should not assume that everyone's Chakras should all be the same as everyone else's; we can accept how they are and accept our impressions of which Chakras require our attention.

And because we know that we can direct the energy using our intent/visualisation, we could always spend some time directing Reiki into a particular Chakra until it seems to be in a better state than before.

Using Visual shortcuts/constructs

The above was a very 'open' way of experiencing someone's Chakras, with no expectations about how they might seem to you. But we can use visual constructs to access intuitive information too: we have already talked about the use if imaginary hands hovering in our mind's eye when we use Reiji ho.

For example, to access intuitive information about someone's chakras in more of a 'controlled' format, you might imagine a mixing desk – like they use in a recording studio – with a series of 'faders' that move up and down a vertical slot. One slider ties in with one Chakra, so you imagine a row of seven 'sliders'.

Look at the slider that ties in with the root Chakra; if it stays half way up, perhaps with a little reassuring 'click' then the Chakra is ok. If it slides down the scale then the Chakra is closed down or spinning sluggishly to the extent that the slider moved down the scale (1 - 100?). If the slider moves up the scale then the Chakra is spinning faster, to the extent that the slider moves up the scale.

Exploring a Chakra's Levels

If you wanted, you could further explore a Chakra, to discover which aspect of the Chakra requires attention. For example, if the Solar Plexus Chakra requires attention then you might want to determine whether it was the physical aspect of the Chakra or the Mental/Emotional aspect that needs to be focused upon. If the latter then it would be appropriate to focus your attention on that Chakra and use energy from SHK - or the Harmony kotodama - as you treat. To deal with the physical aspect then you could use energy from CKR - or the Focus kotodama. To deal with the spiritual aspect then you could imagine that you are channelling a high frequency energy suitable for dealing with the spiritual level; maybe you might choose to use DKM or the empowerment kotodama.

How could you perceive the Chakra's levels? Well you could imagine a sliding scale if you like, with a little pointer that goes up and down the scale. The bottom of the scale represents the physical aspect of the Chakra, and you move through emotions and thoughts to the spiritual aspect. See the diagram below:

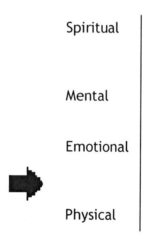

Spiritual

Mental

Emotional

Physical

Focus your attention on a particular Chakra and imagine the sliding scale; see what impression you obtain of the Chakra's needs.

Looking Within

There is no reason why you cannot turn your attention towards your self and your own energy system, your organs and Chakras. Below you can find a few suggestions.

Experiencing One's Chakras

Firstly you can always turn your attention towards your own Chakras, and perceive the state of your own Chakras. Which Chakras require attention, which aspects of the Chakra require attention?

1. Close your eyes.
2. Remind yourself of your connection to the energy through your crown.
3. Imagine energy flooding down to you from above, through the centre of your body to your Tanden.
4. Feel/imagine the energy building up and becoming more intense in your Tanden.
5. Imagine yourself filling with energy.
6. Feel yourself merging with the energy.
7. Consider your chakras; be aware of your chakras. Have no expectations of what you may experience.
8. How do they seem to you?
9. Is your attention pulled towards one or some of them?
10. Do they seem balanced, or do they seem not quite right somehow; in what way?
11. Do this for maybe 5 minutes and feel the flow of energy subside within you; bring yourself back to reality.

You may be surprised to find that you have perceived the Chakras as having quite distinct characteristics compared to each other, and you may have a strong feeling about which Chakras seem fine, which Chakras require some attention, and which ones need boosting rather than restraining.

Internal Scanning by Flooding with Light

Another visual exercise can be used to discern which areas of your self require attention. Imagine that you are flooding yourself with white light, or golden light, and imagine the body filling up with this light, just like water fills a vessel. If you notice any areas where the body does not fill up with light - the liver for example - then this indicates a need for Reiki in that area.

You have scanned your body using your perception focused in a particular way.

Using Intuition and Intent on one's Self

Having determined which areas of your self need attention, you can now focus Reiki on those areas using intent/visualisation.

So for example you can focus the energy on the Chakra using intent/visualisation, and emphasise whichever energy seems appropriate.

Alternatively, you can focus Reiki on the area that would not fill with energy during your internal scanning exercise, treating that area using intention/visualisation until energy flows freely there.

Using a Pendulum

I am not an expert in the use of pendulums, so I would recommend that you read up on the subject – not that I have found a book yet that is particularly useful: most books on pendulums and dowsing seem very preoccupied with finding underground watercourses and mineral deposits!

I can recommend this book though:

> "Anyone Can Dowse for Better Health"
> Arthur Bailey, Quantum Books 1999

You might use a pendulum in a variety of ways:

- To dowse a patient's Chakras in order to establish which are open, which are closed or spinning sluggishly and which are spinning too fast.

- To help with the choice of energy to be channelled into the patient on that particular occasion.

- To establish whether the patient needs to have a further Reiki session.

Introduction to Pendulums

You can use anything that dangles as a pendulum, whether it be a crystal, a ring, a bit of plastic. However, the College of Psychic Studies in Kensington apparently advise people not to use a crystal because it can 'pick up on the subconscious desires and wants of the dowser'. Despite this, I use a crystal and this does not seem to be a problem for me.

'Yes' and 'No' Answers

The first thing to do is to find out what your pendulum does to say 'yes' and 'no'. Try asking 'am I a man?' or 'am I a woman?', blank your mind for a few moments, hold the pendulum away from your body, suspending it from between your thumb tip and index fingertip, and see what it does.

For me, 'yes' is a clockwise movement and 'no' is side-to-side, but it seems to vary from one person to another. You could ask 'show me your yes response' and 'show me your no response' and see what happens. If you try asking 'what should I do now' then you may elicit a response that means ' I can't answer that question with a yes/no'.

The 'Neutral' position

I have found that it is easier for the pendulum to give you answers quickly if it is already moving, rather than holding it still every time whereupon it has to overcome its inertia every time it answers you. In my case I continually swing the pendulum forwards-and-backwards as a 'neutral' position before asking the questions.

Obtaining 'Permission'

Various books recommend that you ask a few questions before entering upon a new endeavour, as follows:

1. Can I do this? (am I able to do this?)
2. Should I do this? (is it right or appropriate for me to do this?)
3. May I do this? (simply politeness really)

If you get 'yes' responses to all the questions then go ahead. If any of the answers are 'no' then don't try any more at that time.

Dowsing Chakras

Ask 'am I able to use this pendulum to dowse the state of a person's Chakras?' If you get a 'yes' response then you can ask these questions:

- What will you show me if the Chakra is open?
- What will you show me if the Chakra is closed or spinning sluggishly?
- What will you show me if the Chakra is spinning too fast?

For me, the responses are my 'yes', 'no' and 'stupid question' responses.

Before you start a treatment, hold the pendulum so that it dangles over the crown Chakra and say to yourself 'show me the state of the crown Chakra' and see what the pendulum does. Then move on to the third eye, throat etc. all the way to the root Chakra.

In fact you do not have to dangle the pendulum over each Chakra; you can happily dowse the Chakras standing by the person's side. In fact you do not have to have the subject in the same room as you, so you can dowse the state of their Chakras before they arrive for the appointment! Within dowsing, it is common for the dowser to have some sort of 'witness' - for example a lock of the person's hair, by way of making a definite connection with the person they are seeking information about. I have not felt the need to do this with Reiki patients, so maybe Reiki and intent is connection enough.

Common Chakra 'presentations'

I have found that it is quite common for the throat, heart and solar plexus Chakras to be closed, which ties in with inability to express oneself and current/long term emotional issues respectively.

I found a closed root Chakra in a girl with anorexia and a lady with multiple addictions.

I found fast-spinning third eye Chakras in a counsellor, research chemist, in a molecular geneticist and a web consultant.

Chakra changes over time

It seems to me that the Chakras do not flap open and shut from one moment to the next, but reflect a general trend within the individual over recent periods of time of variable length, so you are unlikely to see an immediate transformation in their 'Chakra profile' from one treatment to another. However, sometimes an individual Chakra can change from one treatment to another, going from being closed to being open, going from being fast-spinning to being more restrained, and occasionally a Chakra can become closed when it has previously been open, though this is only temporary.

Using the pendulum to look at the state of the Chakras gives you an insight into what is going on in the person at an energetic level, and usually reflects what the person has been telling you about their problem, or gives you a better understanding of what they are experiencing. Interestingly, changes in the Chakra profile can also tie in with the changes that a person reports during a course of treatments, so you can see what is going on underneath, and the differences that these changes produce on the surface.

Moving Beyond Pendulums

On occasion I have forgotten my pendulum by accident, and used an 'imaginary' one instead. I have held my hand in the usual 'holding a pendulum' position and noticed what movements my arm muscles have made my hand produce. Although some people believe that the pendulum moves of its own accord, quite separate from the person holding, I don't believe this: your arm muscles move the pendulum.

The next stage is to go beyond even the pretend pendulum. Some people visualise a pendulum in their heads, and notice how its imaginary swing changes with the questions that are asked.

Other uses during Treatments

Try using a pendulum to obtain advice about which symbol's energy to channel during the treatment you are about to carry out, or to see if you need to carry out a gentle introductory treatment that excludes the use of symbols.

Try asking the pendulum whether the patient needs to come back for another treatment.

Other Questions to ask

Some people use pendulums as a form of 'kinesiology', to find out about any vitamin or mineral deficiencies that they may have, or any food allergies or sensitivities. Try asking these questions about yourself: hold an item of foodstuff and say to yourself "Is it healthy for my body for me to eat this". See what happens.

Students' Experiences

In this section you can read the experiences of some of our 'home study course' students in different parts of the world, talking about their work with intuition. Maybe your experiences will echo theirs, maybe your experiences will be quite different.

"Radiating Reiki produced similar results on all but one of the people I tried it with - that is it made them feel less attached to the experience that had caused them sadness. The one person that differed felt more emotional and vulnerable - she said that the Reiki was giving her sympathy and understanding which she had never had previously for that time in her life. As such she felt she could let the emotion out more - which I suppose was also a process of letting go.

"The Distant Reiji Ho worked as though I was actually present with the person. It really was that good. The power of the mind is amazing. I felt this was an excellent tool (to be interpreted metaphorically) to help understand from the beginning what the subject might not tell you until well into treatments.

"With the Selective Reiji Ho I found that for the area of physical need my hands went to the Solar Plexus area, producing intense heat. The area of mental/emotional need was over the person's knees, while the area of spiritual need hovered over the heart chakra area and shoulders. On consulting afterwards with my recipient she stated that physically she has some digestive problems, mentally/emotionally she is currently making life changing decisions about moving on, while spiritually she feels she need some unconditional and non-judgemental love (not emotional love) as she feels burdened being all things to all people. WOW!

"I have used a pendulum for dowsing chakras and auras now for several years and I find it very effective. The pendulum informs me about all levels - physical, mental, emotional, spiritual, of the person via the different swings it performs over each chakra and around the person. It shows differences in Yin/Yang balances and indicates differences of energy at both conscious/unconscious levels. However, I have never used an imaginary one!

EXCELLENT. I agree with you that it is muscle movements of the arm that make the pendulum work. My sister is a hypnotherapist, and she tells me that this is linked to the unconscious self - and the unconscious self KNOWS because all are one. Looking at chakras was just as exciting. I will be doing this more. In my mind's eye I saw a spinning effect - like a small tornado, but showing different levels of energy, colour, colour intensity, spin, speed, capacity and strength. I found that chakras and pendulum, imaginary or not, distant or not all agreed with each other. A very good exercise, which I will continue to use."

"Radiating Reiki: The first few times I tried this, I found it a little difficult to 'maintain' a flow. I found I could 'connect' with the feelings/thoughts of the other person without much difficulty. But 'sending' the Reiki was where the 'flow' kept feeling interrupted initially, and I felt distracted by the other person's 'state', so found my focus a little hard to maintain. It became a little easier, and more 'fluent' each time I've tried though. So the first two recipients, also had less experiences. In fact the only one was a feeling of warmth, but there wasn't any emotional change. Each time the experiences have been more noticeable, with the warmth being a constant experience, and their focus on the emotional event lessening, and their mood 'lifting'. I found the greatest 'success' with this using it in a 'real' situation unexpectedly though. I was with a friend who was feeling fairly low and negative emotionally. She was talking out her feelings, and I decided to try to radiate Reiki to her while we talked, to see if it would help. Each time she focussed on her negative feelings and thoughts I radiated Reiki, and each time she pulled her thoughts around to a positive point of view and found herself feeling good about things, to the point that she was feeling really uplifted by the end of the evening. I was 'watching' her reactions as they happened, and each time I could see and feel a 'shift' happening in her while I radiated Reiki. I told her what I had been doing afterwards, and she immediately told me that she had felt warmth flowing over and through her periodically throughout the evening and had wondered why! She then looked at the way she had 'turned herself around' and was amazed to realise that each time it had coincided with the warmth she felt too. She realised that her focus hadn't been able to remain with the negative thoughts or emotions each time, and that all she could 'see' were the good/positive results. As you can imagine, I've felt this was far more successful than the arranged practice sessions I did, the results were really noticeable and positive.

"Imaginary Reiji ho: I found my 'imaginary hands' and my real hands drifted to the same areas each time. The 'pull' on my imaginary hands wasn't as strong, but was there, and I'm sure that this will 'strengthen' with more practice. While actually standing next to the person I could also feel a pull on my real hands, so I think this slightly distracted from my imaginary hands, whereas at a distance I have no physical 'presence' to distract me and find it works much

85

better at the moment. I've got past the need to try too hard with Reiji ho too, and have found I feel my hands 'pulled' and just gently drifting into place now because I just 'allow' it to happen instead of trying to focus on or analyse what's going on :o).

"Distant Reiji ho: I found I could do this more 'positively' distantly, mainly I think because I also find remote treatments are something I do intuitively, when I feel the need to, and my physical hands weren't a distraction. I was able to easily 'feel' where my hands wanted to be, more on the level of intuition I think though, as I do with hand positions when I give a remote treatment. I felt a gentle pull and then my hands were in place. I found each time that my hands drifted to areas that I know were consistent with that persons needs at the moment

"Selective Reiji ho: I found this very interesting to do. And some of the results were unexpected initially, but on taking 'the whole picture' they presented it made more sense. There were a few areas of physical need, for instance, that I wouldn't have thought would be physical from what I know of the persons 'problems', but that made sense when I also knew the areas of emotional/mental or spiritual need too. Also, I found some areas needed both physical and emotional, or emotional and spiritual, for instance. I found that very useful too, as it could be 'used' to plan out a course of treatments, if that was appropriate, for someone. I also found it interesting as it could be 'used' to see whether some physical symptoms may have emotional/mental or spiritual 'origins'! I noticed that, while asking to be shown areas of physical need, I could feel earth energy in my hands, and likewise for the others too. It felt as if Reiki was 'setting' the vibration for the 'search' (so to speak). I found this method much better with my real hands, although it still worked with my imaginary hands it wasn't as 'positive' while I was standing near the person physically. Again though I feel it is just a need of practice to 'strengthen' the ability.

"Remote treatment: I was able to 'connect' with the recipient without any problem, and I find that using the connection kotodama makes a 'strong' connection that remains so for the whole treatment. I often find that I use remote treatments, especially for a 'first distant healing' on someone, and use intuitive hand positions. I am able to actually feel as if I'm present in the room with the person I'm treating and 'feel' the flow of Reiki physically, as if I actually was physically with them. I had the same for this treatment too. With this treatment I found that I wanted to concentrate on the person's back, so in my minds eye I was able to turn them over and treat their back directly. The whole treatment was a physical healing, and I found that I used hand positions that mostly concentrated on the spine, and also the full width of the mid-back area. I found myself feeling very warm or hot depending on the amount of Reiki that was being channelled at each hand position, and the flow was very strong. The person involved has a long term problem that gives them nagging back pain almost continually. They have been feeling the pain lessened since the treatment. They also have the added pain of shingles at the moment, and they found this has been greatly relieved since too. All through the treatment they felt a great amount of heat over their back, and felt much

86

more relaxed than they usually can manage, due to the continual back pain, during the treatment they actually found that they felt no pain in their back.

"Also, I've been practising viewing chakras this week, and I think I've found a method which suits me. While trying the sliding scale that you sent me, I though about using traffic lights instead. So, following my 'intuition' I tried it. I'm happy to say that I've had a couple of successes since 'working out' how this would work :o) If I focus on the chakra I'm 'looking' at, and 'see' a set of traffic lights, one of the lights switches on. Similar to with the dowser, I asked which I would be shown for each chakra 'state', and view red as closed/underactive, amber as open, and green as overactive. So I'm well pleased so far, and am looking forward to expanding on this when my friends are back from their holidays :o)"

Western 'Attunements'

 Master Course Audio CD Number 1 - track #10

Background

There are many different attunement methods in existence in the world of Reiki. One can only assume that Mrs Takata taught all her Master students the same ritual, but since then the rituals have evolved and changed, as each teacher has added and deleted various aspects, and emphasised and embellished various parts, and they will have continued to present what they were doing as "Reiki attunements".

In fact Western attunements can now be so different from each other that they are actually contradictory, so if one method works then another method makes no sense by comparison and simply cannot work... and yet all the various Reiki attunements **do** work in practice. So although I recommend that if you are going to carry out an attunement you should follow the instructions you were given, and make sure you are following the instructions correctly, the individual details don't really seem to matter. There are things that you will be doing when you attune that other Reiki Masters will not be doing, and other Reiki Masters will be carrying out various steps that you do not use in your system.

What attunement ritual did Mrs Takata actually teach? Well, I don't think that is completely clear. Maybe the Reiki Alliance has preserved unchanged the original ritual that Mrs Takata taught, but given the $10,000 price tag attached to Alliance Master training I am not so interested in finding out! Actually, I am advised that even within the Reiki Alliance the ritual has been changed as it has been passed form one Master to another, and that some lineages within the Alliance use attunements that are closer to the original than others.

Mrs Takata will have been passing on the attunement ritual that she was taught by Chujiro Hayashi, and I don't think it's clear exactly what that was, either. We have information about a ritual used by one of Dr Hayashi's students - Tatsumi - but there is some controversy within the Reiki world as to whether this is actually an 'attunement' or whether it is some sort of ritual to mark the passage from one teaching level to another.

Recently one of Dr Hayashi's Master students - Mrs Yamaguchi - was discovered in Japan, and some Western Masters have taken training in her "Jikiden" Reiki with her and her son Tadao. She passed away several years ago, though her son Tadao is continuing to offer courses. Interestingly, she seems to have referred to the connection ritual she used as "Reiju", according to someone I spoke to who had trained with her. It seems to have been a fairly simple ritual, too.

But where did Dr Hayashi's attunement method come from? Well, we can be certain that Mikao Usui did not carry out attunements and he did not teach attunements. In fact, it seems that the Imperial Officers had not trained with Usui Sensei long enough to have been taught how to empower others. What they seem to have done is to put together a ritual, in whatever form it took, that gave them the same sort of experience that they had when they were being empowered by Mikao Usui. The Imperial Officers put together a ritual that replicated their experience of empowerment.

I am teaching you an attunement method that has come through to me from William Rand via three intermediate teachers, so what I now have is a slightly distorted or 'mutated' William Rand attunement method. The Rand ritual is quite common within the world of Reiki, and is used for Karuna Reiki attunements too I believe. I do not think Mr Rand developed the ritual by himself, so he will have been passing on what he was taught by his attuning Masters. It is not the most simple attunement method that there is in the world of Reiki, but it is not the trickiest either. It seems to be roughly 'in the middle' in terms of detail/difficulty.

I am teaching you how to attune because every other Reiki Master in the world knows how to carry out attunements. I have to say, though, that you will probably choose in practice to use Reiju empowerments on any First and Second Degree courses that you might run, though a few of my Masters use a combination of attunements and empowerments on their courses. I do recommend that you carry out at least one attunement on any Master course that you host, so that any Masters you teach can say that they have been 'properly' attuned at Master level, even though of course the ritual has no direct connection with what Reiki's founder was doing.

Just to make sure I am making myself clear here, I can say that it is not necessary to use Western attunements at any stage of Reiki teaching: First Degree, Second Degree or Master level. Reiju empowerments are equivalent to attunements in terms of 'connecting' students to the energy, and they can be used instead of them at all levels. In fact, Reiju empowerments produce their own special benefits, and you can read more about that in the "Reiju" section of this manual.

But because Reiki is framed in terms of 'attunements', I am teaching them to you to make sure that this course is compatible with other Reiki Master training courses, and to make sure that you have been 'properly' taught in the minds of the Reiki people who believe that attunements are the 'one true way'. You will also be learning the complete earlier system used by Usui Sensei's surviving students.

Some controversy

There is some controversy in the world of Reiki about the issue of attunements and empowerments. There are some people who are trying to assert that Reiju empowerments are weak and ineffective, that they do not connect you to Reiki properly, and that students are then obliged to keep on having Reiju empowerments again and again in order to 'top up' their ability; the student is said then to be permanently dependent on their teacher.

By way of contrast, Western attunements are presented as the only way to correctly and effectively connect people to Reiki. You do it once and you never need to do it again.

These arguments are, sadly, being put forward for tactical and political reasons. A lot of people within Reiki seem to be quite dogmatic and narrow-minded (this did surprise me a lot!) and believe that what they were taught by their teacher is the one true way, and anyone who does things differently from the way that they were taught isn't doing it properly: they are doing it wrong.

The new information and techniques and approaches that have come from Japan over the last decade or so have been particularly challenging because they have shown that a lot of previously held 'truths' about Reiki are not in fact truths but are just opinions, just ways of practising. The history of Reiki that Mrs Takata was teaching has proved to be not factually correct. The belief that you have to use symbols to connect people to Reiki has gone out of the window. The belief that you have to be attuned to a symbol before it will work for you has turned out not to be correct. The belief that you must use one set of hand positions – "the" hand positions – has been shown to be a very limiting belief.

And if you are a dogmatic and narrow-minded individual, unwilling to embrace new ways of working, unwilling to be open and try new things, resistant to any change, then the best way to deal with challenging information and methods is to attack them and try to denigrate them, rather like people with low self-esteem who make themselves feel better by putting other people down all the time.

It amuses me to see Reiki people trying to argue that empowerments used by Mikao Usui and taught by his surviving students are actually weak and ineffective, and that the only way to properly 'connect' someone is to use connection rituals that were developed by the Imperial Officers after Usui Sensei's death, rituals which were neither used nor taught by Reiki's founder!

According to these people, none of Usui Sensei's surviving students have been properly attuned!

In reality, Reiju empowerments and Western attunements both 'connect' you to Reiki, permanently, though I prefer to see them as allowing you to recognise something that is already there within you, rather than a way of hooking you up to some new energy source that you were not connected to before. Neither system is weak and ineffective, though I can see definite advantages in using Reiju.

In order to be able to practise Reiki long-term, you do not need to have further Reiju empowerments and you do not need to have further Western attunements. However, having said that, there are definite benefits that come through having Reiju again and again, and there would be definite benefits in having Western attunements repeated too. This was a normal part of Reiki practice in Usui's time, but the idea seems to have been lost somewhere along the line as Reiki travelled to the West, and it is only more recently that the idea of repeating attunements has been suggested in the West, by William Rand.

So do not believe everything that you read in books or on Internet discussion groups. Some people have been deliberately twisting things and misconstruing things for their own political purposes, and passing on half-truths to their students by way of presenting their method as the 'one true way'. This is very silly.

Reiki admits of many and varied ways of working and if someone wants to work in a particular way then they can. If someone wants to use standard hand positions that's fine; if someone wants to work intuitively then that's fine, too. If someone wants to use Reiju they can and if they want to use Western attunements they can. What we should not tolerate is one group trying to impose their beliefs on others.

Making Sense of Attunements

When I was taught to carry out attunements I was taught the three different attunement levels together in one go, with what seemed to be endless different instructions that varied from one level to another, with no rhyme or reason to the process. It made no sense: point 1 do this, point 2... point 25... point 37 etc. To try and get my head around the instructions I laid them all down on the floor in front of me and looked to see if I could find the similarities and differences between the different attunements.

I found that one section at the beginning was the same no matter what level you were attuning at, so I called that section "Setting the Scene"; the section that followed was basically the same too, and that could be called "Opening the Student up"; the next section – which was the section that varied from one level to another – I referred to as "Putting the Symbols In"; the final section – again basically the same from one level to another – I called "Closing Things Down".

By breaking the attunement sequence down into manageable chunks, and by looking at the similarities and differences between different attunements, the sequences became a lot easier to learn and understand, so that is the format that we are going to follow here and this approach works well in practice. We will **not** be learning all the attunement sequences at the same time: we will focus on Second Degree as an example of how to attune, and once that has been learned and understood then we can move on to learn Master attunements. If you know how to attune at Second Degree level then Master attunements make sense and are easy.

Finally we will look at the First Degree attunements, which don't fit quite so well with the general attunement scheme you'll be learning, but which will make a lot more sense once you are comfortable with attuning at Second Degree and Master level.

Though they are detailed, with quite a few steps to go through and remember, attunements do have a certain logic to them, which helps you to make sense of them. Every other Reiki teacher on the planet has learned how to carry out attunements, and you can learn too.

Basic Attunement Format

Our Western attunements, at whatever level, can be broken down into four distinct stages:

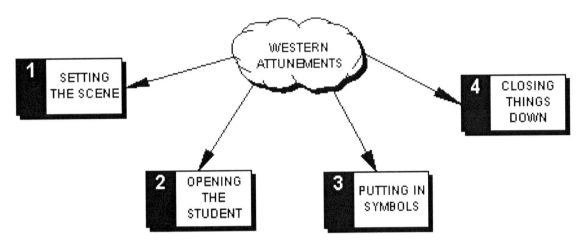

You will be going through these four stages whenever you carry out attunements at First Degree, Second Degree or Master Levels. The only stage that varies significantly from one level to another is Stage 3: "Putting in the Symbols", though the other stages vary slightly from one level to another, and Stage 2 is a little different at First Degree. You'll find out all about that later.

Shortly we will be going through a Second Degree attunement in more detail, but before we do that we need to introduce you to an energy exercise that you will be carrying out when you perform these Western attunements...

The Microcosmic Orbit and the Violet Breath

There are two techniques that seem to turn up in a lot of Western attunement methods: the use of the Microcosmic orbit, and the 'violet breath'. Interestingly, neither of these techniques appear in the Japanese empowerments that have come through to the West.

The **microcosmic orbit** consists of the functional and governor channels (meridians) running in the midline along the front and back of the body. Once these two meridians are connected, it is said that you become a stronger channel for Reiki, whether carrying out a treatment or performing an attunement. The use of the Hui Yin circuit is included on our Second-Degree courses, and is mentioned below.

The **violet breath** technique is a way of transmitting Reiki energy during an attunement, using the breath, though it is not carried out in all attunement styles. It is interesting that although the use of breath to transfer energy seems quite common in Western attunements, not many people seem to have used breath as a way of conveying Reiki during treatments, though we now know that this is a technique used in Japanese 'Gakkai' Reiki.

The Huiyin point

Below is an explanation of what and where the Huiyin point is, what you have to do with it and why. When you gently contract your Huiyin (basically your pelvic floor) and press your tongue to the roof of your mouth, you make an energy circuit that prevents Reiki from leaking out elsewhere. This means that if you are treating someone when the circuit is made, you will be channelling the maximum amount of Reiki through your hands, and you may be able to feel an increase in the tingling from your hands, which corresponds with you having made the circuit. Contracting your Huiyin consistently does take a bit of practice, but it does get easier with repetition.

Another important point about the Huiyin is that it is contracted throughout the Western attunement process in the style that you will be learning. If you are going to be a Reiki Master and attune people in the Western system, you will have to be able to contract your Huiyin for fairly long periods of time! Having a strong pelvic floor is a good thing in life!

Here is the explanation from my original manual. Overleaf is a diagram to show where the Huiyin can be located.

> "The utilisation of the Huiyin energy centre to link the chakras and endocrine glands in order to produce a spiritual transformation has been employed by initiates for thousands of years. Using the Huiyin point and the 'Governor channel' can produce the 'Raku' energy up through the spine and into the brain.
>
> The Huiyin point or perineum is located at the pressure point that is felt as a small hollow between the anus and the genitals. The Huiyin point needs to be contracted as if trying to pull the point up gently into the body and held. Frequent practice will allow the point to be contracted for considerable lengths of time.
>
> When giving attunements a high frequency Ki energy enters your system and passes through the Huiyin point; contraction of the Huiyin point maintains the energy in the body and prevents Ki from escaping."

It is suggested that to practise contracting the Huiyin, you should attempt at first to make the contractions maybe twenty times in quick succession, and then try to hold the contraction for as long as possible. It is usual to experience some frustration or discomfort at first. Try to hold the Huiyin contraction throughout daily activities. Do remember that a very gentle contraction is required.

It is important to hold the Huiyin contraction throughout the entire attunement process. Eventually you will only need to focus on the Huiyin for an effective contraction to take place.

The subtle body channels originate at the Huiyin point and provide a circuit from the Governor channel at the back of the body, to the Functional channel at the front. To complete the circuit, press the tongue to the roof of the mouth during the contraction, maintaining pressure against the roof of your mouth throughout. It is sometimes possible to feel an energy rush as the circuit is completed.

The location of the Huiyin point is illustrated below, together with a diagram to show the position and course of the Conception Vessel.

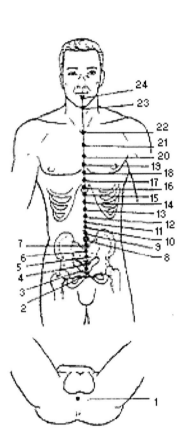

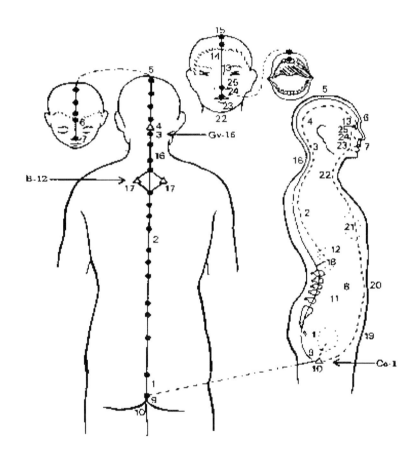

The Violet Breath

The 'Violet breath' is an integral part of the Western attunement process you are learning, though it is not present in all styles. It is used to transfer Reiki energy, together with the Tibetan Master Symbol, into the crown of the student being attuned.

The whole process will need regular practice to become effective, but the results in terms of energy accumulation and transfer are said to be 'outstanding', according to my original Master manual. The violet breath becomes easier to do the more you do it.

Basically, you are breathing normally in and out, but as you breathe you imagine that energy is moving round your body along a particular circuit, and accumulating in one place. Here are the instructions...

1   Contract the Huiyin and place your tongue to the roof of your mouth. Keep them there throughout the procedure.

2   Inhale deeply, expanding the lower abdomen, and imagine air as a white mist entering the crown Chakra, moving through the tongue and down the Functional channel (along the front of the body) to collect at the Huiyin point.

3   While you pause before exhaling, see the breath rise up the spine along the Governor channel (along the back of the body) to the centre of the head.

4   As you exhale, imagine the white mist spinning clockwise in the head and allow the white mist to turn blue, and then a clear violet.

5   Hold this image.

6   Repeat Instructions 2 – 5 twice more, at least, each time adding more energy to the energy that is already spinning in your head. You continue to breathe in and out throughout this repeated procedure, moving energy in time with your in-breaths and out-breaths.

7   Within the violet light, visualise the Tibetan Master symbol and say its name three times to empower it.

The Second Degree Attunement

 Master Course Audio CD Number 2 - track #2

 DVD Video sequence

How Many Second Degree Attunements Should I Give?

If you were attuned in the Western method during your Second Degree training, you will probably have received two attunements. They are both the same, repeated to 'make doubly sure' that you are well and truly attuned at Second Degree level. It is nice to do it more than once, and I used to carry out two of these attunements on my Second Degree courses when I used Western attunements.

In some lineages students will receive just one attunement at Second Degree level.

There is also a less common system where people receive one attunement for each symbol, I believe, making three attunements for Reiki Second Degree.

How Long Should I Leave Between Attunements?

In some lineages people are taught a specific time that has to be left between attunements: one hour, four hours or whatever. I do not think such restrictions are useful or necessary, though it would be nice to space the attunements out during the course. When I used Western attunements on my Second Degree course I used to do one attunement in the morning and one in the afternoon, for example.

Now I use Reiju empowerments on both my First Degree and Second Degree courses; I carry three of these out during the morning of each course, and there is roughly an hour between each one, but I do not believe the time left between each one is too significant.

First, let us remind ourselves of the general scheme for carrying out any attunement:

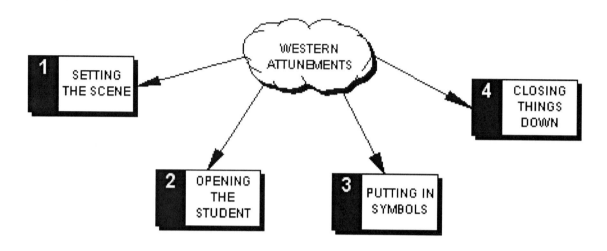

The detailed instructions you will find below are framed in terms of attuning a group of students. You do **not** do a complete attunement for each student, finish with them, and then move on to the next. What you do is to begin the attunement for the first student, going only so far through the sequence, and then you move on to the next student and carry out the same part of the sequence, until all students have received that stage of the attunement process. Then you carry out the next stage of the attunement for each student in turn, and so on.

During the attunements you will be standing behind each student in turn to begin with, the attunement then moves round to the front of each student in turn, and finally you finish off the attunement by standing behind each student in turn again.

So rather like entertainers on television who balance spinning plates on the end of a pointed stick, when you attune a group of people you 'get each person going' in turn, and come back to them at intervals to keep their attunement going.

Here is a brief overview of the four stages, followed by the detailed instructions...

Setting the Scene

Here you focus your attention on the attunement to follow, open up your energy system to Reiki and create a sacred space by drawing symbols in the air, drawing the energy of the Reiki symbols into the room, flooding the room with light.

SACRED SPACE

Opening the Student

Here you connect to the student, build up the violet breath, and you transmit the two Master symbols into the student's head, blowing the "Tibetan" Master symbol in, and drawing the Usui Master symbol above the crown.

Putting the Symbols In

Here you insert the symbols that you are going to "attune" the student to, so for example during the Second Degree attunements you "attune" the student to CKR, SHK and HSZSN by inserting these three symbols into different parts of the student:

(1) into their hands/crown with their hands held above their head

(2) into their third eye

(3) into their palms with their hands held out in front of them.

 ### Closing Things Down

Here you carry out various visualisations and affirmations to emphasise that the effects of the attunement are sealed in and that the attunement is permanent; both the student and teacher are blessed by this process.

Setting the Scene – detailed instructions

This is the first stage of carrying out any attunement, and the ritual is done once, no matter how many people are sitting before you waiting to receive their attunements. You will be calling higher powers for help, focusing on what attunement you wish to carry out, you will fill your hands with the energy of the Usui Master Symbol (UMS). You will open your energy centres using CKR, and create a sacred space by drawing various symbol in the air. This stage culminates in your connecting the Hui Yin circuit, and this connection is then maintained throughout the attunement ritual. You can stand anywhere you like in the room when you carry out this stage.

Here the stages are summarised:

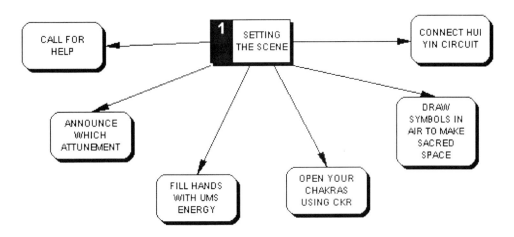

Here are the step-by-step instructions for the "Setting the Scene" Stage:

1. Say a silent prayer, calling on Mikao Usui, the Ascended Masters and any Deity you would like to attend, to be present, during the attunement. Maybe ask for the help of your spiritual guides and the Reiki guides.
2. Silently state that this is to be a Reiki II attunement.
3. Draw the Usui DaiKoMyo on your palm, saying the name three times, and press your palms together three times to 'transfer the effect across' to the other palm.
4. Draw ChoKuRei over each chakra, starting with the crown and finishing with the root chakra, and then over your whole chakra system, to empower and open yourself.
5. Draw Reiki symbols in the air, intending that their energy floods the room, creating sacred space. Visualise the symbols in violet as if on a great screen in the middle of the room, and say their names three times, mantra style, to empower them. Use this order... Tibetan DaiKoMyo, Usui DaiKoMyo, HSZSN, SHK, CKR.
6. Contract the Huiyin, place the tongue to the top of the mouth. Remember to hold these connections throughout the entire attunement process.

Call on Mikao Usui and Ascended Masters to attend.

Say to yourself that this is to be a Second Degree Attunement.

Fill your hands with energy from Usui Master Symbol: draw symbol over palm and say its name 3 times

Press palms together 3 x to transfer effect across .

Open your chakras by drawing CKR over each chakra in turn from the crown to the root.

Follow this by drawing a large CKR over your whole chakra system.

Draw the two Master symbols and the three Second Degree symbols in the air, for each one saying its name three times.

Flood the symbols' energies into the room.

Connect the Huiyin circuit.

Draw the Fire Dragon down the student's back, from the crown to the root charka

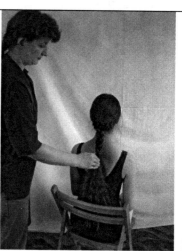

Opening the Student - detailed instructions

This Stage is the same when attuning at Second Degree and Master levels, and differs a little at First Degree. You will be opening and balancing the student's chakras by using the Fire Dragon symbol, connecting to them, and building up the violet breath. You will put the "Tibetan" Master Symbol (TMS) in the energy that you have accumulated in your head, blowing this symbol and the accumulated energy into the student's crown, and then you will follow that by drawing the Usui Master Symbol (UMS) in the air above the crown, sending that symbol into the crown too. You will be standing behind the student throughout this stage.

Here the stages are summarised:

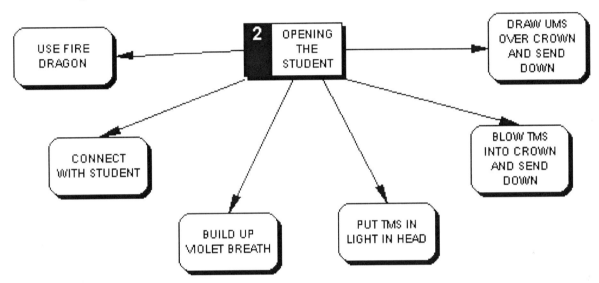

Here are the step-by-step instructions for the "Opening the Student" Stage:

1. Move towards your first student and stand behind them. Draw the Fire Serpent from the student's crown, down to the base of the spine/root chakra.
2. Place both hands on the shoulders and close your eyes to gain rapport with the student.
3. Build up the Violet Breath, with each new breath adding more energy to the energy that is already spinning in your head. When you feel ready, visualise the Tibetan DaiKoMyo within the violet light, and say the name three times.
4. Place your hands on the student's crown; open your hands to breathe the Tibetan DaiKoMyo and the violet light into the student's crown chakra. Use the index finger of your hand as a guide to help you imagine the symbol moving through the head to the base of the brain, while repeating the name **Dai Ko Myo** three times to yourself, in mantra style.
5. Draw the Usui DaiKoMyo over the head and, using the index finger of one of your hands as a guide, imagine the symbol moving into the crown chakra and through the head to the base of the brain, while repeating the name **Dai Ko Myo** three times to yourself, in mantra style.

Hands on shoulders. Connect to the student.

Build up the Violet Breath.

Draw energy through your crown and down the front as you breathe in, the energy rises up the back and it enters your head as you exhale. The energy starts spinning.

With each new breath add a bit more energy to the energy that is already spinning in your head.

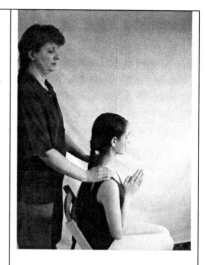

Visualise TMS in Violet light, and say name 3 x

Blow symbol and energy into crown.

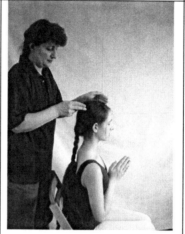

Send the Symbol/energy to base of skull/head

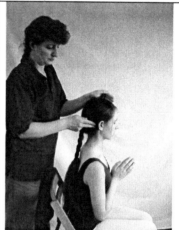

Use index finger as a guide to help you imagine

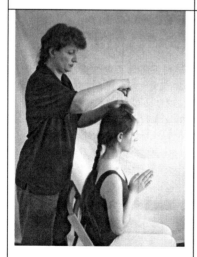

Draw UMS in air over crown and say name 3 x

Send the Symbol thro' crown to base of skull

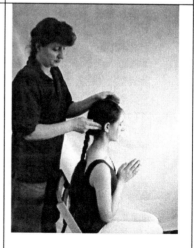

Use index finger as a guide to help you imagine

Putting the Symbols In – detailed instructions

This Stage is the one that differs from one attunement to another. We are learning a Second Degree attunement at the moment, and this is the stage where we put the three Second Degree symbols into the student – "attuning" the student to these symbols, if you will. This stage is carried out with you standing behind the student to begin with, and then you move round to the front of them.

NOTE: We now know that you do not need to be attuned to symbols in order to be connected to Reiki, and we know that you do not need to be 'attuned' to a symbol for a symbol to be effective, but Western attunements are all framed in terms of 'attuning' the student to the Reiki symbols.

You are going to be putting the Second Degree symbols into three places: into the student's hands which are held above their crown, then into the student's third eye, and then into the student's palms (with their hands held out in front of them). Once you have done this you will press the student's palm chakras to 'activate' them and blow energy from the hands up and down their chakras, using a particular sequence/direction.

Here the stages are summarised:

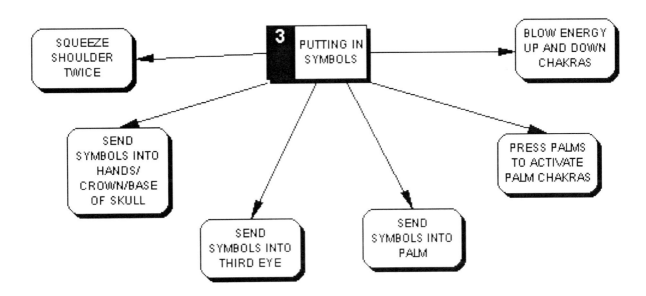

1. Squeeze the student's left shoulder, which is the cue to raise their hands to the top of their head. If they don't respond to the signal, then reach forwards and guide their hands to the right position yourself.
2. Hold your student's hands in place over their crown using one hand, and draw HonShaZeShoNen in the air above their fingers. Using your index finger as a guide, imagine the symbol moving into the hands, through the crown chakra to the base of the brain, while repeating the symbol name **Hon Sha Ze Sho Nen** three times to yourself in mantra style.

3. Draw SeiHeKi in the air over their fingers. Using your right hand as a guide, picture the symbol moving into the hands, through the crown chakra to the base of the brain, while repeating the symbol name **Sei He Ki** three times to yourself in mantra style.
4. Draw ChoKuRei in the air over their fingers. Using your right hand as a guide, picture the symbol moving into the hands, through the crown chakra to the base of the brain, while repeating the symbol name **Cho Ku Rei** three times to yourself in mantra style.
5. Move the student's hands from the top of their head back down to the prayer position.

Go on to the next person, until all your students have received this part.

6. Move to your student's front and open their hands out flat, overlapping one on the other, holding one hand under the student's hands to support them.
7. Draw HonShaZeShoNen in front of their Third Eye chakra, tapping towards their third eye three times with your fingers, while visualising the symbol moving into the Third Eye and saying the symbol name **Hon Sha Ze Sho Nen** to yourself three times in mantra style.
8. Draw SeiHeKi in front of their Third Eye chakra, tapping towards their third eye three times with your right hand, while visualising the symbol moving into the Third Eye and saying the symbol name **Sei He Ki** to yourself three times in mantra style.
9. Draw ChoKuRei in front of their Third Eye chakra, tapping towards their third eye three times with your right hand, while visualising the symbol moving into the Third Eye and saying the symbol name **Cho Ku Rei** to yourself three times in mantra style.
10. Draw HonShaZeShoNen in the air above their hands. Picture the symbol moving into the hands while repeating the symbol name **Hon Sha Ze Sho Nen** to yourself three times in mantra style. Tap the palm as you say each name. Three taps in total.
11. Draw SeiHeKi in the air above their hands. Picture the symbol moving into the hands while repeating the symbol name **Sei He Ki** to yourself three times in mantra style. Tap the palm three times.
12. Draw ChoKuRei in the air above their hands. Picture the symbol moving into the hands while repeating the symbol name **Cho Ku Rei** to yourself three times in mantra style. Tap the palm three times.
13. Press both palms with your thumbs to activate the palm chakras.
14. Place the student's hands together in the prayer position. Let go of their hands. Blow the energy from the hands down to the base chakra, up the body to the crown, down the body to the base, and up to the hands again.

Go on to the next person, until all your students have received this part.

Squeeze one shoulder twice. Student brings hands above crown.

Hold hands in place over the crown

Send the three Second Degree symbols, in turn, into the hands, crown and take them down to the base of the skull.

Draw each symbol in the air above the fingers, say the name three times, and move your index finger to help you imagine the symbol passing down into the head.

Do this for CKR, SHK and HSZSN...

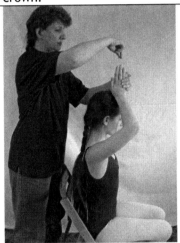

Draw the symbol and say its name 3 times

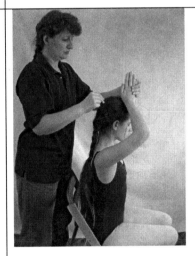

Use finger as a guide as you send symbol down

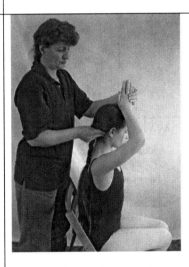

... to the base of the skull, into the head

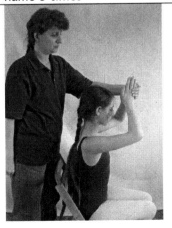

Move their hands forward, back into prayer position

Move round in front of the person and take hold of their hands.

Fold their hands open and rest one hand on the other.

Support their hand with one hand; you will be drawing symbols with your other hand.

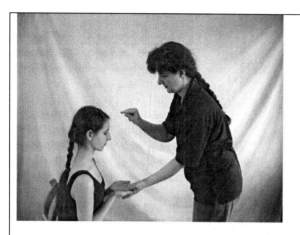

Send the three Second Degree symbols, in turn, into the third eye. Draw each symbol in front of the third eye, say the name three times, and as you 'tap' the name, imagine the symbol passing into the 3rd eye.

Do this for CKR, SHK and HSZSN...

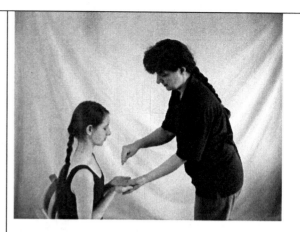

Now turn your attention to the hands. Send the three Second Degree symbols, in turn, into the hands. Draw each symbol above the palm, say the name three times, and as you 'tap' the name, tap the palm.

Do this for CKR, SHK and HSZSN...

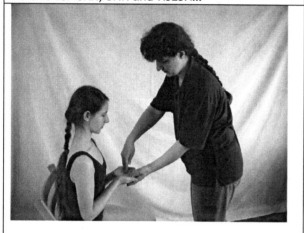

(tapping the palm)

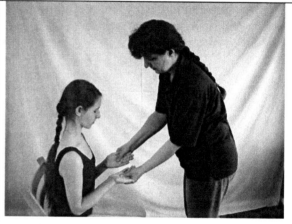

Move the hands apart and press palms three times using your thumbs. Return hands to prayer position

Now you are going to be blowing energy from the hands, up and down the chakras.

1. Blow from the hands to the root chakra.
2. Blow from the root to the crown chakra.
3. Blow from the crown to the root chakra.
4. Blow from the root to the hands.

Move round the back of the person again.

Closing Things Down – detailed instructions

This Stage is basically the same from one attunement to another. It is a little tricky because you have to learn some "affirmations" that you say silently as you go through the ritual. You will remember them quickly and easily.

You are going to imagine a ball of light entering the student's heart Chakra and affirming that they are a successful and confident Reiki healer. You will be using a visualisation of a door and CKR and affirmations that emphasise to yourself that the attunement process is permanent, you will be affirming that both the student and teacher are blessed by the attunement process, and you will be saying a silent "thank you" to the higher powers that you invited to attend at the start of the attunement sequence. This stage is carried out standing behind the student until right at the end, where you move the student's hands down into their lap and the attunement sequence finishes.

Here the stages are summarised:

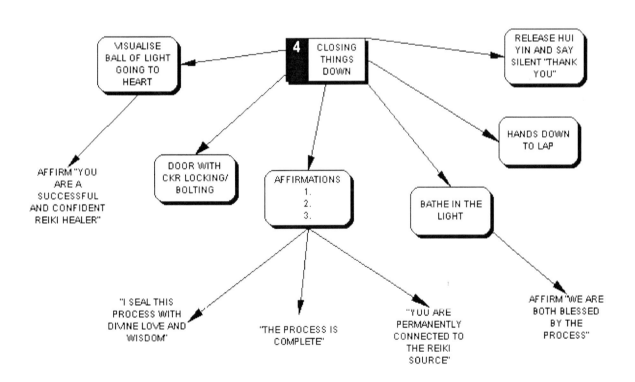

1. Move to your student's back and place your hands on their shoulders for a few moments, to gain rapport again. Look down through the crown chakra and see a ball of white light moving into the heart chakra. Say to yourself "I visualise a ball of light entering the heart chakra". State a positive affirmation to yourself, three times. Intend the affirmation to be accepted in their heart. Try this: "You are a successful and confident Reiki healer".
2. Place your thumbs at the base of their skull and say to yourself "I seal this process with divine love and wisdom", while imagining a door with ChoKuRei on it being closed and locked. Say to yourself "the process is complete" and "you are permanently connected to the Reiki source".
3. Place your hands back on the student's shoulders and say to yourself "We are both blessed by this process". Imagine a shaft of brilliant white light shining down onto yourself and the student. Bathe in the light.

Go on to the next person, until all your students have received this part.

4. Move to the front of your student and place their hands on their legs, palms down.
5. Move back so that you are facing all your students, and thank the guides etc that you invited at the start of the procedure. Hold your hands at waist level with your palms facing your students, exhale, and release the Huiyin and tongue.
6. Ask the students to take a few long deep breaths and to come back slowly and open their eyes.

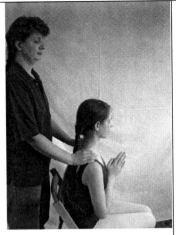 Hands on the shoulders.	Visualise a ball of brilliant white light going through the crown down to the heart Chakra. Say an affirmation that you intend is going to be accepted in their heart. Say (silently): "you are a successful and confident Reiki healer"	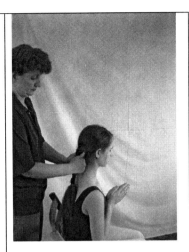 Rest the thumbs against the base of the skull
	Visualise a door with CKR on it. See the door shutting, locking, and bolting. Say (silently): "I seal this process with divine love and wisdom." "The process is complete." "You are permanently connected to the Reiki source."	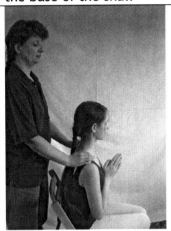 Hands back on shoulders
Visualise a shaft of brilliant white light shining down on yourself and the person in front of you. Bathe in the light. Say (silently): "We are both blessed by this process" Move in front of the person and place their hands in their lap, palms down.		Take a step back, face the student, and hold your palms towards them, as shown. Take a deep breath; release Huiyin/tongue. Say a mental 'thank you' to the people you invited to attend at the beginning of the attunement. Ask the student to take a deep breath and slowly bring themselves back, and open their eyes.

A Few Practical Points

Here are just a few practical points to bear in mind when carrying out Western attunements, to help the process flow smoothly, comfortably and quickly for yourself and the student.

Drawing the Reiki Symbols

You do not need to draw out the symbols like a draughtsman or an architect. They do not need to be a precise work of art that takes 5 minutes for each symbol. They can be drawn fairly quickly and that works perfectly well. Equally, you do not need to use super-speed, with your hand movements a blur, but find a brisk comfortable speed. You can't see the symbol that you have just drawn; the important thing is that you know what the symbol looks like, you know what you are aiming to draw; make the hand movements with that goal in mind.

Sending the Symbols into the Crown / Base of Skull

You are simply using your index finger as a guide to help you imagine that the symbols are passing through the crown and into the base of the skull/brain. Do this gently and lightly. You do not need to bore your fingertip into the back of their head at the end of the symbol's journey, and you do not need to trace a groove down the length of their head in time with the symbol's journey!

Sending the Symbols into the Third Eye and Palms

Make sure that you do not tap the third eye when you send the symbols in; 'tap' the air as you say the symbols' name and imagine that they are passing into the third eye. When sending the symbols into the palm, gently but firmly tap the centre of the palm as you say the symbols' name; do not 'whack' the symbol into the palms!

111

Blowing energy up and down the Chakras

As you blow energy up and down the Chakras you do not need to bend in half in order to do this: you do not need to position your mouth in front of the entire length of the person's Chakra system/spine. Simply stand in front of the person – not too close - and blow up and down the Chakras from a distance. You do not need to contort yourself as you do this; you will be simply moving your head/shoulders a little.

Reiki Master Attunement

How Many Master attunements should I give?

Although there is only one Master attunement, it is nice to repeat it, just like we can repeat the Second-Degree attunements. When I used only Western attunements I used to carry out the Master attunement twice on the Master course. Now I use one Master attunement and three 'Master level' Reiju empowerments.

Differences between Master and Second Degree attunements

Since you are now familiar with attunements at Second Degree level it would be useful if we focus on the differences between Second Degree and Master attunements. The differences are as follows:

Setting the Scene

State that this is to be a **Reiki Master attunement**, not a Second Degree attunement.

Opening the Student Up

No difference. Perform this stage as before.

Putting the Symbols In

Here you put in these symbols into the three places (hands above head - third eye - palms):

1. Tibetan Master Symbol
2. Usui Master Symbol
3. HSZSN
4. SHK
5. CKR

So you insert all the symbols that they have had so far: the three Second Degree symbols and the two Master symbols... and any other symbols you might like to 'attune' the recipient to, for example the Fire Dragon, Heart Chakra symbol etc.

Closing Things Down

Affirm that the student is a "Successful and Confident Reiki **Master**"

Below you can read the detailed Master attunement instructions, again broken down into the four stages that you are familiar with...

Setting the Scene

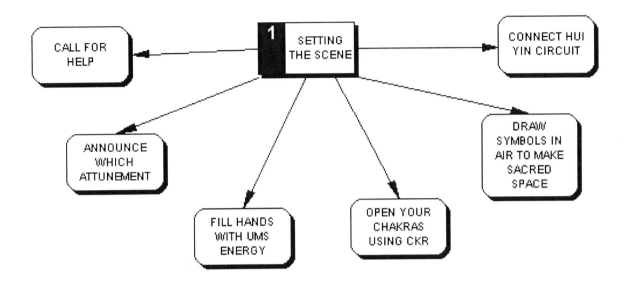

1. Say a silent prayer, calling on Mikao Usui, the Ascended Masters and any Deity you would like to attend, to be present, during the attunement. Maybe ask for the help of your spiritual guides and the Reiki guides.
2. Silently state that this is to be a Reiki Master attunement.
3. Draw the Usui DaiKoMyo on your palm, saying the name three times, and press your palms together three times to 'transfer the effect across' to the other palm.
4. Draw ChoKuRei over each chakra, starting with the crown and finishing with the root chakra, and then over your whole chakra system, to empower and open yourself.
5. Draw Reiki symbols in the air, intending that their energy floods the room, creating sacred space. Visualise the symbols in violet as if on a great screen in the middle of the room, and say their names three times, mantra style, to empower them. Use this order... Tibetan DaiKoMyo, Usui DaiKoMyo, HSZSN, SHK, CKR.
6. Contract the Huiyin, place the tongue to the top of the mouth. Remember to hold these connections throughout the entire attunement process.

Opening the Student

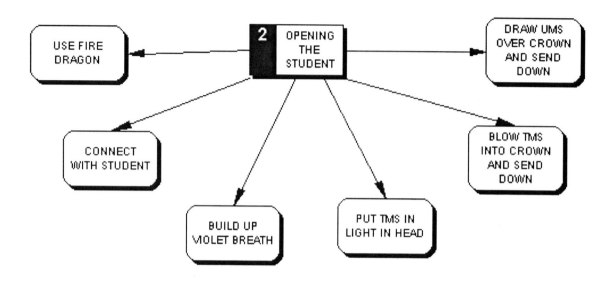

1. Move towards your first student and stand behind them. Draw the Fire Serpent from the student's crown, down to the base of the spine/root chakra.
2. Place both hands on the shoulders and close your eyes to gain rapport with the student.
3. Build up the Violet Breath, with each new breath adding more energy to the energy that is already spinning in your head. When you feel ready, visualise the Tibetan DaiKoMyo within the violet light, and say the name three times.
4. Place your hands on the student's crown; open your hands to breathe the Tibetan DaiKoMyo and the violet light into the student's crown chakra. Use the index finger of your hand as a guide to help you imagine the symbol moving through the head to the base of the brain, while repeating the name **Dai Ko Myo** three times to yourself, in mantra style.
5. Draw the Usui DaiKoMyo over the head and, using the index finger of one of your hands as a guide, imagine the symbol moving into the crown chakra and through the head to the base of the brain, while repeating the name **Dai Ko Myo** three times to yourself, in mantra style.

Putting the Symbols In

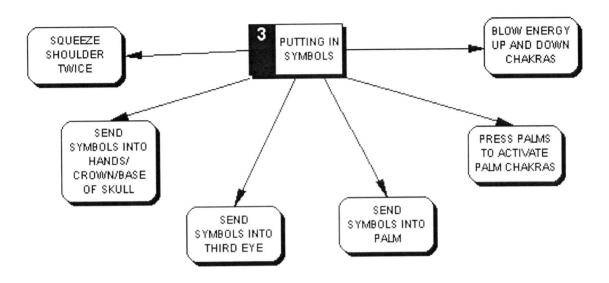

1. Squeeze the student's left shoulder, which is the cue to raise their hands to the top of their head. If they don't respond to the signal, then reach forwards and guide their hands to the right position yourself.
2. Hold your student's hands in place over their crown using one hand, and draw the Tibetan DaiKoMyo in the air above their fingers. Using your index finger as a guide, imagine the symbol moving into the hands, through the crown chakra to the base of the brain, while repeating the symbol name **Dai Ko Myo** three times to yourself in mantra style.
3. Draw the Usui DaiKoMyo in the air over their fingers. Using your index finger as a guide, picture the symbol moving into the hands, through the crown chakra to the base of the brain, while repeating the symbol name **Dai Ko Myo** three times to yourself in mantra style.
4. Draw HonShaZeShoNen in the air over their fingers. Using your index finger as a guide, picture the symbol moving into the hands, through the crown chakra to the base of the brain, while repeating the symbol name **Hon Sha Ze Sho Nen** three times to yourself in mantra style.
5. Draw SeiHeKi in the air over their fingers. Using your index finger as a guide, picture the symbol moving into the hands, through the crown chakra to the base of the brain, while repeating the symbol name **Sei He Ki** three times to yourself in mantra style.
6. Draw ChoKuRei in the air over their fingers. Using your index finger as a guide, picture the symbol moving into the hands, through the crown chakra to the base of the brain, while repeating the symbol name **Cho Ku Rei** three times to yourself in mantra style.
7. Move the student's hands from the top of their head back down to the prayer position.

Go on to the next person, until all your students have received this part.

8. Move to your student's front and open their hands out flat, overlapping one on the other, holding one hand under the student's hands to support them.
9. Draw the Tibetan DaiKoMyo in front of their Third Eye chakra, tapping towards their third eye three times with your fingers, while visualising the symbol moving into the Third Eye and saying the symbol name **Dai Ko Myo** to yourself three times in mantra style.
10. Draw the Usui DaiKoMyo in front of their Third Eye chakra, tapping towards their third eye three times with your right hand, while visualising the symbol moving into the Third Eye and saying the symbol name **Dai Ko Myo** to yourself three times in mantra style.
11. Draw HonShaZeShoNen in front of their Third Eye chakra, tapping towards their third eye three times with your right hand, while visualising the symbol moving into the Third Eye and saying the symbol name **Hon Sha Ze Sho Nen** to yourself three times in mantra style.
12. Draw SeiHeKi in front of their Third Eye chakra, tapping towards their third eye three times with your right hand, while visualising the symbol moving into the Third Eye and saying the symbol name **Sei He Ki** to yourself three times in mantra style.
13. Draw ChoKuRei in front of their Third Eye chakra, tapping towards their third eye three times with your right hand, while visualising the symbol moving into the Third Eye and saying the symbol name **Cho Ku Rei** to yourself three times in mantra style.
14. Draw the Tibetan DaiKoMyo in the air above their hands. Picture the symbol moving into the hands while repeating the symbol name **Dai Ko Myo** to yourself three times in mantra style. Tap the palm as you say each name. Three taps in total.
15. Draw the Usui DaiKoMyo in the air above their hands. Picture the symbol moving into the hands while repeating the symbol name **Dai Ko Myo** to yourself three times in mantra style. Tap the palm three times.
16. Draw HonShaZeShoNen in the air above their hands. Picture the symbol moving into the hands while repeating the symbol name **Hon Sha Ze Sho Nen** to yourself three times in mantra style. Tap the palm three times.
17. Draw SeiHeKi in the air above their hands. Picture the symbol moving into the hands while repeating the symbol name **Sei He Ki** to yourself three times in mantra style. Tap the palm three times.
18. Draw ChoKuRei in the air above their hands. Picture the symbol moving into the hands while repeating the symbol name **Cho Ku Rei** to yourself three times in mantra style. Tap the palm three times.
19. Press both palms with your thumbs to activate the palm chakras.
20. Place the student's hands together in the prayer position. Let go of their hands. Blow the energy from the hands down to the base chakra, up the body to the crown, down the body to the base, and up to the hands again.

Go on to the next person, until all your students have received this part.

Closing Things Down

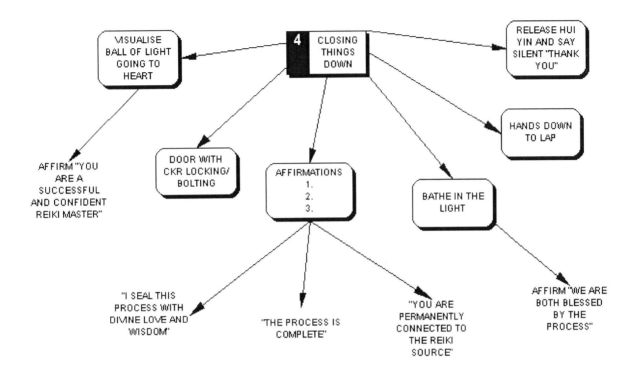

1. Move to your student's back and place your hands on their shoulders for a few moments, to gain rapport again. Look down through the crown chakra and see a ball of white light moving into the heart chakra. Say to yourself "I visualise a ball of light entering the heart chakra". State a positive affirmation to yourself, three times. Intend the affirmation to be accepted in their heart. Try this: "You are a successful and confident Reiki Master".

2. Place your thumbs at the base of their skull and say to yourself "I seal this process with divine love and wisdom", while imagining a door with ChoKuRei on it being closed and locked. Say to yourself "the process is complete" and "you are permanently connected to the Reiki source".

3. Place your hands back on the student's shoulders and say to yourself "We are both blessed by this process". Imagine a shaft of brilliant white light shining down onto yourself and the student. Bathe in the light.

Go on to the next person, until all your students have received this part.

4. Move to the front of your student and place their hands on their legs, palms down.

5. Move back so that you are facing all your students, and thank the guides etc that you invited at the start of the procedure. Hold your hands at waist level with your palms facing your students, exhale, and release the Huiyin and tongue.

6. Ask the students to take a few long deep breaths and to come back slowly and open their eyes.

First Degree Attunements

How Many First Degree attunements should I give?

In the world of Western Reiki these has for a long time been a notion that there have to be four attunements for Reiki First Degree, and a few years ago it was not uncommon for potential Reiki students to enquire how many attunements a teacher carried out on the First Degree course, since four attunements were seen as the proper number: any less and it wasn't being done 'properly'.

This is a big historical mistake. Mikao Usui carried out endless empowerments on his students, and when you trained with him it was rather like martial arts training, so the student moved on to the next training level when it was thought they had developed sufficiently. Dr Hayashi did not teach Reiki in the same way: he taught First Degree over five days I believe, 90 minutes per day for five days. During that time he carried out four connection rituals, because it is nice to do a few and because the number four probably fitted in nicely with his schedule. As that passed through Mrs Takata to the West it ended up as "thou shalt do four attunements for Reiki First Degree".

In view of this, it is not surprising to find that we will be carrying out four attunements at Reiki First Degree level. In fact there are three slightly different First Degree attunements to learn, with the third one repeated so that adds up to the magic number four. These attunements don't fit so well with the 'logic' of the Second Degree and Master attunements, so we have left them to last.

Differences between First and Second Degree attunements

You are already familiar with attunements at Second Degree level, so it would be useful if we focus on the differences between these attunements and attunements at First Degree level. The differences are as follows:

Setting the Scene

State that this is to be a **First Degree attunement**, not a Second Degree attunement.

Opening the Student Up

There is an important difference here. It is not only the two Master symbols that are inserted here. After the Usui Master Symbol is drawn over the crown and sent down, SHK and HSZSN are drawn over the crown and inserted in the same way. You do this progressively, though, adding one more symbol to this stage each time you do another First Degree attunement. The table below should make this clear.

This is how it looks:

Which attunement are we talking about?	What goes into the crown, during the "Opening the Student Up" stage?	What goes into the three places: (1) hands held above the head, (2) third eye, (3) palms held in front of the student?
1st Reiki 1 attunement	Tibetan DKM Usui DKM	CKR
2nd Reiki 1 attunement	Tibetan DKM Usui DKM **SeiHeKi**	CKR
3rd Reiki 1 attunement	Tibetan DKM Usui DKM **SeiHeKi** **HonShaZeShoNen**	CKR
4th Reiki 1 attunement This is just a repeat of the 3rd attunement	Tibetan DKM Usui DKM **SeiHeKi** **HonShaZeShoNen**	CKR

... so in the 1st of the First Degree attunements, you send the two Master symbols into the crown and use only CKR in the three places (hands/3rd eye/hands)

In the 2nd of the First Degree attunements, you send the Master symbols **and SeiHeKi** into the crown and use only CKR in the three places (hands/3rd eye/hands)

In the 3rd of the First Degree attunements, you send the Master symbols **and SeiHeKi and HonShaZeShoNen** into the crown and use only CKR in the three places (hands/3rd eye/hands)

This can be interpreted as making each attunement 'stronger' because you are adding another symbol whenever you do another of the First Degree attunements.

Putting the Symbols In

During all the First Degree attunements you put CKR into the three places (hands above head – third eye – palms). CKR is the only symbol to go into these places.

Closing Things Down

No difference. Perform this stage as for Second Degree.

Below you can read the detailed First Degree attunement instructions, again broken down into the four stages that you are familiar with...

Attunement #1

1   Say a silent prayer, calling on Mikao Usui, the Ascended Masters and any Deity you would like to attend, to be present, during the attunement. Maybe ask for the help of your spiritual guides and the Reiki guides.

2   Silently state that this is to be a Reiki I attunement.

3   Draw the Usui DaiKoMyo on your palm, saying the name three times, and press your palms together three times to 'transfer the effect across' to the other palm.

4   Draw ChoKuRei over each chakra, starting with the crown and finishing with the root chakra, and then over your whole chakra system, to empower and open yourself.

5   Draw Reiki symbols in the air, intending that their energy floods the room, creating sacred space. Visualise the symbols in violet as if on a great screen in the middle of the room, and say their names three times, mantra style, to empower them. Use this order... Tibetan DaiKoMyo, Usui DaiKoMyo, HSZSN, SHK, CKR.

6   Contract the Huiyin, place the tongue to the top of the mouth. Remember to hold these connections throughout the entire attunement process.

7   Move towards your first student and stand behind them. Draw the Fire Serpent from the student's crown, down to the base of the spine/root chakra.

8   Place both hands on the shoulders and close your eyes to gain rapport with the student.

9   Build up the Violet Breath, with each new breath adding more energy to the energy that is already spinning in your head. When you feel ready, visualise the Tibetan DaiKoMyo within the violet light, and say the name three times.

10 Place your hands on the student's crown; open your hands to breathe the Tibetan DaiKoMyo and the violet light into the student's crown chakra. Use the index finger of your hand as a guide to help you imagine the symbol moving through the head to the base of the brain, while repeating the name **Dai Ko Myo** three times to yourself, in mantra style.

11 Draw the Usui DaiKoMyo over the head and, using the index finger of one of your hands as a guide, imagine the symbol moving into the crown chakra and through the head to the base of the brain, while repeating the name **Dai Ko Myo** three times to yourself, in mantra style.

12 Squeeze the student's left shoulder, which is the cue to raise their hands to the top of their head. If they don't respond to the signal, then reach forwards and guide their hands to the right position yourself.

13 Hold your student's hands in place over their crown using one hand, and draw ChoKuRei in the air above their fingers. Using your index finger as a guide, imagine the symbol moving into the hands, through the crown chakra to the base of the brain, while repeating the symbol name **Cho Ku Rei** three times to yourself in mantra style.

14 Move the student's hands forwards from the top of their head back down to the prayer position.

Go on to the next person, until all students have received this part.

15   Move to your student's front and open their hands out flat, overlapping one on the other, holding one hand under the student's hands to support them.

16   Draw ChoKuRei in front of their Third Eye chakra, tapping towards their third eye three times with your fingers, while visualising the symbol moving into the Third Eye and saying the symbol name **Cho Ku Rei** to yourself three times in mantra style.

17   Draw ChoKuRei in the air above their hands. Picture the symbol moving into the hands while repeating the symbol name **Cho Ku Rei** to yourself three times in mantra style. Tap the palm as you say each name. Three taps in total.

18   Press both palms with your thumbs three times, to activate the palm chakras.

19   Place the student's hands together in the prayer position. Let go of their hands. Blow the energy from the hands down to the base chakra, up the body to the crown, down the body to the base, and up to the hands again.

Go on to the next person, until all students have received this part.

20   Move to your student's back and place your hands on their shoulders for a few moments, to gain rapport again. Look down through the crown chakra and see a ball of white light moving into the heart chakra. Say to yourself "I visualise a ball of light entering the heart chakra". State a positive affirmation to yourself. Intend the affirmation to be accepted in their heart. Try this: "You are a successful and confident Reiki healer".

21   Place your thumbs at the base of their skull and say to yourself "I seal this process with divine love and wisdom", while imagining a door with ChoKuRei on it being closed and locked. Say to yourself "the process is complete" and "you are permanently connected to the Reiki source".

22   Place your hands back on the student's shoulders and say to yourself "We are both blessed by this process". Imagine a shaft of brilliant white light shining down onto yourself and the student. Bathe in the light.

Go on to the next person, until all students have received this part.

23   Move to the front of your student and place their hands on their legs, palms down.

24   Move back so that you are facing all your students, and thank the guides etc that you invited at the start of the procedure. Hold your hands at waist level with your palms facing your students, exhale, and release the Huiyin and tongue.

25   Ask the students to take a few long deep breaths and to come back slowly and open their eyes.

Attunement #2

1. Say a silent prayer, calling on Mikao Usui, the Ascended Masters and any Deity you would like to attend, to be present, during the attunement. Maybe ask for the help of your spiritual guides and the Reiki guides.
2. Silently state that this is to be a Reiki I attunement.
3. Draw the Usui DaiKoMyo on your palm, saying the name three times, and press your palms together three times to 'transfer the effect across' to the other palm.
4. Draw ChoKuRei over each chakra, starting with the crown and finishing with the root chakra, and then over your whole chakra system, to empower and open yourself.
5. Draw Reiki symbols in the air, intending that their energy floods the room, creating sacred space. Visualise the symbols in violet as if on a great screen in the middle of the room, and say their names three times, mantra style, to empower them. Use this order... Tibetan DaiKoMyo, Usui DaiKoMyo, HSZSN, SHK, CKR.
6. Contract the Huiyin, place the tongue to the top of the mouth. Remember to hold these connections throughout the entire attunement process.
7. Move towards your first student and stand behind them. Draw the Fire Serpent from the student's crown, down to the base of the spine/root chakra.
8. Place both hands on the shoulders and close your eyes to gain rapport with the student.
9. Build up the Violet Breath, with each new breath adding more energy to the energy that is already spinning in your head. When you feel ready, visualise the Tibetan DaiKoMyo within the violet light, and say the name three times.
10. Place your hands on the student's crown; open your hands to breathe the Tibetan DaiKoMyo and the violet light into the student's crown chakra. Use the index finger of your hand as a guide to help you imagine the symbol moving through the head to the base of the brain, while repeating the name **Dai Ko Myo** three times to yourself, in mantra style.
11. Draw the Usui DaiKoMyo over the head and, using the index finger of one of your hands as a guide, imagine the symbol moving into the crown chakra and through the head to the base of the brain, while repeating the name **Dai Ko Myo** three times to yourself, in mantra style.
12. Draw SeiHeKi over the head and, using your right hand as a guide, picture the symbol moving into the crown chakra and through the head to the base of the brain, while repeating the name **Sei He Ki** three times to yourself, in mantra style.
13. Squeeze the student's left shoulder, which is the cue to raise their hands to the top of their head. If they don't respond to the signal, then reach forwards and guide their hands to the right position yourself.
14. Hold your student's hands in place over their crown using one hand, and draw ChoKuRei in the air above their fingers. Using your index finger as a guide, imagine the symbol moving into the hands, through the crown chakra to the base of the brain, while repeating the symbol name **Cho Ku Rei** three times to yourself in mantra style.
15. Move the student's hands from the top of their head back down to the prayer position.

Go on to the next person, until all students have received this part.

16. Move to your student's front and open their hands out flat, overlapping one on the other, holding one hand under the student's hands to support them.
17. Draw ChoKuRei in front of their Third Eye chakra, tapping towards their third eye three times with your fingers, while visualising the symbol moving into the Third Eye and saying the symbol name **Cho Ku Rei** to yourself three times in mantra style.
18. Draw ChoKuRei in the air above their hands. Picture the symbol moving into the hands while repeating the symbol name **Cho Ku Rei** to yourself three times in mantra style. Tap the palm as you say each name. Three taps in total.
19. Press both palms with your thumbs to activate the palm chakras.
20. Place the student's hands together in the prayer position. Let go of their hands. Blow the energy from the hands down to the base chakra, up the body to the crown, down the body to the base, and up to the hands again.

Go on to the next person, until all students have received this part.

21. Move to your student's back and place your hands on their shoulders for a few moments, to gain rapport again. Look down through the crown chakra and see a ball of white light moving into the heart chakra. Say to yourself "I visualise a ball of light entering the heart chakra". State a positive affirmation to yourself, three times. Intend the affirmation to be accepted in their heart. Try this: "You are a successful and confident Reiki healer".
22. Place your thumbs at the base of their skull and say to yourself "I seal this process with divine love and wisdom", while imagining a door with ChoKuRei on it being closed and locked. Say to yourself "the process is complete" and "you are permanently connected to the Reiki source".
23. Place your hands back on the student's shoulders and say to yourself "We are both blessed by this process". Imagine a shaft of brilliant white light shining down onto yourself and the student. Bathe in the light.

Go on to the next person, until all students have received this part.

24. Move to the front of your student and place their hands on their legs, palms down.
25. Move back so that you are facing all your students, and thank the guides etc that you invited at the start of the procedure. Hold your hands at waist level with your palms facing your students, exhale, and release the Huiyin and tongue.
26. Ask the students to take a few long deep breaths and to come back slowly and open their eyes.

Attunement #3

1. Say a silent prayer, calling on Mikao Usui, the Ascended Masters and any Deity you would like to attend, to be present, during the attunement. Maybe ask for the help of your spiritual guides and the Reiki guides.
2. Silently state that this is to be a Reiki I attunement.
3. Draw the Usui DaiKoMyo on your palm, saying the name three times, and press your palms together three times to 'transfer the effect across' to the other palm.
4. Draw ChoKuRei over each chakra, starting with the crown and finishing with the root chakra, and then over your whole chakra system, to empower and open yourself.
5. Draw Reiki symbols in the air, intending that their energy floods the room, creating sacred space. Visualise the symbols in violet as if on a great screen in the middle of the room, and say their names three times, mantra style, to empower them. Use this order... Tibetan DaiKoMyo, Usui DaiKoMyo, HSZSN, SHK, CKR.
6. Contract the Huiyin, place the tongue to the top of the mouth. Remember to hold these connections throughout the entire attunement process.
7. Move towards your first student and stand behind them. Draw the Fire Serpent from the student's crown, down to the base of the spine/root chakra.
8. Place both hands on the shoulders and close your eyes to gain rapport with the student.
9. Build up the Violet Breath, with each new breath adding more energy to the energy that is already spinning in your head. When you feel ready, visualise the Tibetan DaiKoMyo within the violet light, and say the name three times.
10. Place your hands on the student's crown; open your hands to breathe the Tibetan DaiKoMyo and the violet light into the student's crown chakra. Use the index finger of your hand as a guide to help you imagine the symbol moving through the head to the base of the brain, while repeating the name **Dai Ko Myo** three times to yourself, in mantra style.
11. Draw the Usui DaiKoMyo over the head and, using the index finger of one of your hands as a guide, imagine the symbol moving into the crown chakra and through the head to the base of the brain, while repeating the name **Dai Ko Myo** three times to yourself, in mantra style.
12. Draw HonShaZeShoNen over the head and, using your right hand as a guide, picture the symbol moving into the crown chakra and through the head to the base of the brain, while repeating the name **Hon Sha Ze Sho Nen** three times to yourself, in mantra style.
13. Draw SeiHeKi over the head and, using your right hand as a guide, picture the symbol moving into the crown chakra and through the head to the base of the brain, while repeating the name **Sei He Ki** three times to yourself, in mantra style.
14. Squeeze the student's left shoulder, which is the cue to raise their hands to the top of their head. If they don't respond to the signal, then reach forwards and guide their hands to the right position yourself.
15. Hold your student's hands in place over their crown using one hand, and draw ChoKuRei in the air above their fingers. Using your index finger as a guide, imagine the symbol moving into the hands, through the crown chakra to the base of the brain, while repeating the symbol name **Cho Ku Rei** three times to yourself in mantra style.
16. Move the student's hands from the top of their head back down to the heart.

Go on to the next person, until all your students have received this part.

17. Move to your student's front and open their hands out flat, overlapping one on the other, holding one hand under the student's hands to support them.
18. Draw ChoKuRei in front of their Third Eye chakra, tapping towards their third eye three times with your fingers, while visualising the symbol moving into the Third Eye and saying the symbol name **Cho Ku Rei** to yourself three times in mantra style.
19. Draw ChoKuRei in the air above their hands. Picture the symbol moving into the hands while repeating the symbol name **Cho Ku Rei** to yourself three times in mantra style. Tap the palm as you say each name. Three taps in total.
20. Press both palms with your thumbs to activate the palm chakras.
21. Place the student's hands together in the prayer position. Let go of their hands. Blow the energy from the hands down to the base chakra, up the body to the crown, down the body to the base, and up to the hands again.

Go on to the next person, until all your students have received this part.

22. Move to your student's back and place your hands on their shoulders for a few moments, to gain rapport again. Look down through the crown chakra and see a ball of white light moving into the heart chakra. Say to yourself "I visualise a ball of light entering the heart chakra". State a positive affirmation to yourself, three times. Intend the affirmation to be accepted in their heart. Try this: "You are a successful and confident Reiki healer".
23. Place your thumbs at the base of their skull and say to yourself "I seal this process with divine love and wisdom", while imagining a door with ChoKuRei on it being closed and locked. Say to yourself "the process is complete" and "you are permanently connected to the Reiki source".
24. Place your hands back on the student's shoulders and say to yourself "We are both blessed by this process". Imagine a shaft of brilliant white light shining down onto yourself and the student. Bathe in the light.

Go on to the next person, until all your students have received this part.

25. Move to the front of your student and place their hands on their legs, palms down.
26. Move back so that you are facing all your students, and thank the guides etc that you invited at the start of the procedure. Hold your hands at waist level with your palms facing your students, exhale, and release the Huiyin and tongue.
27. Ask the students to take a few long deep breaths and to come back slowly and open their eyes.

Summary of Attunements

Below you can see a "Mind Map" showing the main points of your Western attunements, and below that you can find some single-sheet summary sheets based on a few key words. They should provide a useful 'trigger'.

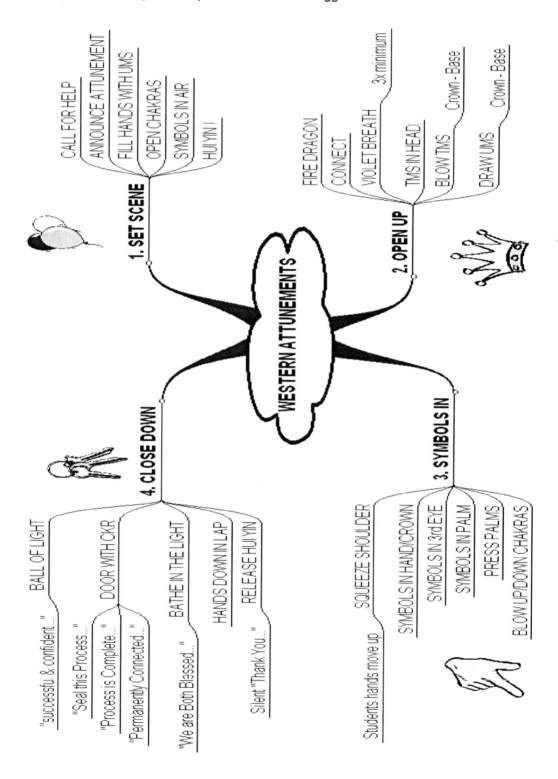

Attunement Summary Sheets

Reiki Second Degree

Setting the Scene

- Call for help/Announce what Attunement
- Usui DKM on palms
- CKR on chakras
- Symbols in the air
- Huiyin / tongue

Opening the Student Up

- Draw Fire Dragon
- Connect
- Build up Violet breath
- Transmit violet breath & Tibetan DKM
- Usui DKM into head

Putting the Symbols In

- Hands above head   HSZSN, SHK, CKR
- Third Eye   HSZSN, SHK, CKR
- Open palms   HSZSN, SHK, CKR
- Press Palm Chakras
- Blow up and down chakras

Closing Things Down

- Ball of light affirmation
- Door/CKR visualisation
- Seal this process... process is complete... permanently connected
- We are both blessed/bathe in the light
- Hands on Lap
- Release Hui Yin/Silent "Thank You"

Reiki Master attunement

Setting the Scene

- Call for help/Announce what Attunement
- Usui DKM on palms
- CKR on chakras
- Symbols in the air
- Huiyin / tongue

Opening the Student Up

- Draw Fire Dragon
- Connect
- Build up Violet breath
- Transmit violet breath & Tibetan DKM
- Usui DKM into head

Putting the Symbols In

- Hands above head

  Tibetan DKM
  Usui DKM
  HSZSN, SHK, CKR
  ...plus any other symbols

- Third Eye

  Same symbols as above

- Open palms

  Same symbols as above

- Press Palm Chakras
- Blow up and down chakras

Closing Things Down

- Ball of light affirmation
- Door/CKR visualisation
- Seal this process... process is complete... permanently connected
- We are both blessed/bathe in the light
- Hands on Lap
- Release Hui Yin/Silent "Thank You"

Reiki First Degree

Setting the Scene

- Call for help/Announce what Attunement
- Usui DKM on palms
- CKR on chakras
- Symbols in the air
- Huiyin / tongue

Opening the Student Up

- Draw Fire Dragon
- Connect
- Build up Violet breath
- Transmit violet breath & Tibetan DKM
- Usui DKM into head

Now transmit these symbols into crown...

Attunement:	First	Second	Third	Fourth
	None Extra	SHK	SHK HSZSN	SHK HSZSN

Putting the Symbols In

- Hands above head   CKR
- Third Eye   CKR
- Open palms   CKR
- Press Palm Chakras
- Blow up and down chakras

Closing Things Down

- Ball of light affirmation
- Door/CKR visualisation
- Seal this process... process is complete... permanently connected
- We are both blessed/bathe in the light
- Hands on Lap
- Release Hui Yin/Silent "Thank You"

Students' Experiences

In this section you can read the experiences of some of our 'home study course' students in different parts of the world, talking about their work with attunements. Maybe your experiences will echo theirs, maybe your experiences will be quite different.

"I think I feel reasonably comfortable with the Second Degree attunements now but I will continue with this until I am very familiar with it before I move on to the 1st and Master practice. I found the Huiyin contraction uncomfortable at first, and even 'forgot' it half way through, but it seems to be getting easier. Also I found I forgot to keep my tongue in place while I blew the energy into the chakras - well practice makes perfect. I practised some of these attunements with my sister, we received our 1st and 2nd levels together - and she said that these practice sessions had been as good as, if not better, for her. She could feel the energy entering her crown, 3rd eye and hands on each occasion.

"The violet breath experience is quite amazing - you can actually feel the spin of energy and see the colour change as it occurs. And I saw a door with CKR burnt into the wood and could hear the closing and locking sounds! I really did feel blessed by the process. Giving the attunement was a better experience for me than my own 1st and 2nd level attunements. I really felt connected."

"My first reaction while watching the DVD was 'I'll never remember all that!'...but I'm glad to say that I now feel comfortable with the Reiki 2 and the Master's attunement 'sequence' and can remember each 'step' :o), though I think it will be a little longer before I can fully remember the first degree one's without referring to the summary sheet for which symbols to 'use'. Again, I've enjoyed it, even though it appeared far more daunting at the beginning than any of the other stages of the course so far.

"For me personally I would say this has been the most challenging (especially memory wise....LOL) and complicated part of the course so far. So, being the logical minded person that I am, I actually broke down the practice sessions into parts for the first two days before even attempting the whole 'process' in one, firstly watching the video while trying to maintain the Huiyin/tongue connection, and separately practicing the attunement sequence along with the

video (then the audio track), and also separately practicing the violet breath. I've done this all a couple of times each day :o) By doing it this way it has, for me, made the learning process easier. (Something which I'm always in favour of!) I'm not yet able to maintain the Huiyin/tongue connection for the full length of the attunement, which doesn't really surprise me personally, as I have always found it difficult to maintain for more than 3 or 4 minutes without a great deal of concentration, (which I've always found has then distracted me from the actual energy flow) so as yet I haven't been able to 'do' a 'full' attunement on my prop without having to 're-connect' several times. Again though, I am sure that practice will enable me to do this, as over the week I have managed to increase that time by continually practicing while doing other things, as you suggest. So although I can't yet maintain the connection long enough, I am beginning to find that it takes less effort and concentration, which to me is a positive step :o). I also am beginning to notice an 'energy drop' when I 'lose' the connection. Again I find this positive as it means I'm no longer needing to concentrate all my attention on maintaining the connection too.

"For the first few days I found that building the violet breath caused me rather a nasty headache until I released it too, the level of energy felt so intense and while I was 'spinning' it in my head I felt as if I was spinning too. I am naturally a slow, deep breather, and I've often found that breathing techniques can have a slightly adverse effect on me until I 'accustom' myself to them. So, I've practiced this separately all week too, starting with two or three shorter breaths to begin with, and allowing the energy to dissipate when it became uncomfortable, to the point where I can now build it without any discomfort breathing in my normal way, and complete the visualisation of the Tibetan DKM and blowing it into the crown. It still feels as if my head will explode with the amount of energy that builds though, but is now, at least, not painful! And also, as the week has gone on, I've found that the 'level' of energy that I am able to build is becoming more intense. While practising I have been releasing the energy to the universe, but yesterday and today I've also found that it leaves me with a 'high', spaced out feeling until I ground myself! As I will continue to practice this separately, I'm now realising that I need to use the energy that I build in some way when not using it for attunements.

"So, the attunements 'make sense' and I feel comfortable with them. I can 'perform' the sequences for second degree and Masters attunements from memory, and the first degree by referring to the summary sheet before each one, so to speak. I can build up the violet breath, and maintain the Huiyin/tongue connection long enough to be able to complete the opening up stage of the attunement, without any difficulty. I take longer for each stage than on the video sequence, but that I'm sure again, will flow more easily with practice (and also once I stop mixing up my DKM with my HSZSN!! Which unfortunately I have found myself doing this week!!...LOL) I'm sure I'll get my fuddled brain around them properly soon though, (well I certainly hope so!!). But I've managed to have a laugh at myself over it, and I'm so glad that only my teddy bear has been there to see me doing that...LOL!

132

"As this week has been a more 'mentally' oriented part of the course, I've found that I haven't as yet, reached the point where I can 'feel' what's happening during the attunement. Yes, I feel Reiki flowing through me, but my focus is still very much mentally on the 'process'. So, I'm looking forward to being able to flow through the attunement 'process' and feel involved in the actual attunement more than I can at present."

Attuning to Other Symbols

On the Master course you will have been attuned to the following symbols, and the attunement instructions in this manual provide you with detailed instructions on how to attune others to these symbols:

- 'Tibetan' Master Symbol
- Usui Master Symbol
- Hon Sha Ze Sho Nen
- Sei He Ki
- Cho Ku Rei

All these symbols were inserted into your hands (held above your head), your third eye, and into your hands (held out in front of you). However, you have also been attuned to other symbols that are not mentioned specifically in the instructions:

- The Fire Dragon
- The Spirit Column
- The Mental Spiral
- The Heart Chakra Symbol
- Simon Treselyan's 'Grace' Symbol
- The Taoist version of the 'Grace' symbol
- The Emotional Butterfly

This section tells you how to do this.

When I carried out the Reiki Master attunements on you, as well as the first five symbols, I also inserted the other symbols into your hands (held above your head), into your third eye, and into your palms (held out in front of you). Most of the new symbols do not have names that are repeated as a mantra (the Heart Chakra Symbol being an exception to this).

To attune you to the Heart Chakra Symbol I did exactly the same thing that is done with all the other 'symbols with names':

1. I drew out the symbol, said its name three times, and visualised the symbol passing through your hands into the base of your brain (using a finger as a visual guide that ends up touching the back of your neck)
2. I drew out the symbol, said its name three times, and visualised the symbol passing into your third eye

133

3. I drew out the symbol, said its name three times, and visualised the symbol passing into your palms. I tapped your palms three times as I repeated the symbols' name to myself.

You know how to do that.

For the symbols that do not have names, I simply drew out the symbols, and imagined them passing into your hands/brain, your third eye, and your palms, using a gentle hand movement to send the symbols on their way, but without touching or tapping.

Do we need to 'attune' to a symbol?

A Basic Belief of Western Reiki

It has been a basic tenet of Western-style Reiki that the Reiki symbols are useless unless you have been attuned to them: they won't work until after the Second Degree course. There was no way that people could actually prove this, though, because nobody knew of a way to attune people without using symbols, and no-one really got to try out the symbols before the day of the Reiki 2 course. A few things have happened to me to make me realise that this basic principle of Western Reiki is not correct, though I think that there will be a lot of people who will find this difficult to accept.

Symbols work for Reiki 1 people

On my Reiki 2 courses I now send the symbols out in advance, and also provide people with information about how the symbols are used in practice. Some Reiki 1 people have been trying out the symbols before coming on the Reiki 2 course, and they have found that the symbols 'worked', and produced the same effects that the students got when they went through the Reiki 2 training day. These Reiki 1 students had been attuned using the Western-style Reiki 1 attunement process - which does involve the use of symbols - so it could be said that they were still 'attuned' to the symbols to some degree. Thus this evidence was not yet conclusive.

Symbols work even when you are not attuned to them

However, I have now had the opportunity to take people to Reiki Second Degree level using Japanese Reiju empowerments for Reiki 1, and Reiju with Kotodama for Reiki 2. None of these attunements involve the use of symbols, so the students were 'untainted' by any Reiki symbol. I found that the symbols were working for them even before the day of the Reiki 2 course - they played around with them based on the information that I sent them prior to the Reiki 2 course. When they came on the Reiki 2 course proper they had exactly the same experiences when using the symbols as my students had 6 months previously, for example, when I was using the Western-style attunements throughout.

Conclusion

The above proves to me that Reiki is the energy, and that when you are attuned to Reiki, it is the energy that you are attuned to. The symbols are a way of representing different aspects of that energy, and so long as you are attuned to the energy then the symbols will work for you even if you have not been 'attuned' to them. There are other ways of representing the energy: symbols from other cultures, prayers, and direct intent. Reiki and the symbols are separate things, and the symbols are not the energy.

Interestingly, Usui did not attune his students to the Reiki symbols. They were given the symbols and learned to 'become' the energies through meditation.

Healing Attunements

'Healing Attunements' seem to have originated with William Rand, a prominent American Reiki Master. They are described as a way of 'breaking down blockages' or breaking down an individual's resistance to the flow of Reiki. Thus they would be appropriate when a person does not seem to be receiving the benefits that Reiki seems to produce in almost everyone.

But I feel a bit uncomfortable with this view. My impression is that the idea of such 'resistance' or 'blockages' is not appropriate: Reiki flows whenever you place your hands on someone, and if they do not show an improvement then that is happening for other reasons, for example their karmic need to experience a condition, or if they are clinging onto a condition subconsciously because it serves some need that they have (though I believe that Reiki can deal with this).

I am uneasy about this idea of blockages that Reiki will not shift, and 'bringing in the heavy guns' to deal with the blockage. That seems to be imposing your will, whereas the frame of mind we need to cultivate when we practise Reiki is of detachment, sending the energy in a neutral way – with a loving, compassionate intent certainly – rather than imposing our preferred result on the situation. We can learn to do some things that seem to make treatments more effective, maybe, and we can learn to work with the energy in terms of intuitive hand positioning and allowing intuition to guide us in terms of what energy/symbol we are focusing on... but that is different from striding in with our big armaments and 'forcing' a result.

If it's not going to work then it's not going to work, and that sometimes does happen.

I suppose you could see healing attunements as a sort of 'Reiki blessing', and that they should be seen as a way of bringing the light of Reiki into a person's heart and soul. They are not attuned to Reiki, but the energy is brought deep within them. Thus healing attunements might be used in the sort of circumstances where you would choose to give treatments using the two Master symbols.

In practice, though, I would recommend giving someone a Reiju empowerment as part of their treatment, so that they can use the energy on themselves between appointments. This is apparently what Usui used to do quite routinely, and if they wanted to take things further then they could start some long-term 'formal' training with him. I would not use the healing attunement in practice, but I have included it in this manual for completeness. For me the most interesting aspect of healing attunements is contained in the next paragraph, where the instructions begin...

Instructions

"Ask the client to describe the issue or condition they would like healed, and ask them where in the body they believe the condition to be residing. Next, ask the client to identify a shape, colour, texture, weight, and even smell, of the condition to be removed. If the client has difficulty finding an area, ask for a guess. There is no 'wrong' answer and they do not have to answer all the questions."

1. Say a silent prayer, asking for the help of your spiritual guides and the Reiki guides.
2. Silently state that this is to be a healing attunement.
3. Draw the Usui DaiKoMyo on your palms.
4. Draw ChoKuRei on each chakra and over the whole body, to empower and open yourself.
5. Draw the Reiki symbols in the air, intending their power to fill the room. Visualise the symbols in violet as if on a great screen in the middle of the room, and say their names three times, mantra-style, to empower them. Use this order... Tibetan DKM, Usui DKM, HSZSN, SHK, CKR.
6. Contract the Huiyin, place the tongue to the top of the mouth. Remember to hold the Huiyin throughout the entire process.
7. Move towards your first client and stand behind them. Draw the Fire Serpent from the top of the client's head, down the spine.
8. Place both hands on the shoulders and close your eyes to gain rapport with the client.
9. Produce the Violet Breath, visualise the Tibetan DKM within the violet light.
10. Place your hands on the client's crown, opening your hands to breathe the Tibetan DKM and violet light into the client's crown chakra. Use your right hand as a guide and picture the symbol moving through the head to the heart chakra, while repeating the name **Dai Ko Myo** three times to yourself, in mantra style.
11. Draw the Usui DKM over the head and, using your finger as a guide, picture the symbol moving into the crown chakra and through the head to the heart chakra, while repeating the name **Dai Ko Myo** three times to yourself, in mantra style.
12. Draw HSZSN over the head and, using your finger as a guide, picture the symbol moving into the crown chakra and through the head to the heart chakra, while repeating the name **Hon Sha Ze Sho Nen** three times to yourself, in mantra style.
13. Draw SHK over the head and, using your finger as a guide, picture the symbol moving into the crown chakra and through the head to the heart chakra, while repeating the name **Sei He Ki** three times to yourself, in mantra style.
14. Draw CKR over the head and, using your finger as a guide, picture the symbol moving into the crown chakra and through the head to the heart chakra, while repeating the name **Cho Ku Rei** three times to yourself, in mantra style.

15. Move to your client's front and draw the Usui DKM over the crown chakra. Using your finger as a guide, picture the symbol moving through the brow chakra, the heart chakra, and into the solar plexus, while repeating the symbol name **Dai Ko Myo** three times to yourself in mantra style. Gently tap the top of the head three times.
16. Draw HSZSN over the crown chakra. Using your finger as a guide, picture the symbol moving through the brow chakra, the heart chakra, and into the solar plexus, while repeating the symbol name **Hon Sha Ze Sho Nen** three times to yourself in mantra style. Gently tap the top of the head three times.
17. Draw SHK symbol over the crown chakra. Using your finger as a guide, picture the symbol moving through the brow chakra, the heart chakra, and into the solar plexus, while repeating the symbol name **Sei He Ki** three times to yourself in mantra style. Gently tap the top of the head three times.
18. Draw CKR over the crown chakra. Using your finger as a guide, picture the symbol moving through the brow chakra, the heart chakra, and into the solar plexus, while repeating the symbol name **Cho Ku Rei** three times to yourself in mantra style. Gently tap the top of the head three times.
19. Blow from the solar plexus down to the base chakra, up the body to the crown, down the body to the solar plexus and back to the crown again. On the last upward blow, use your hands to lift out all the negative energy and throw it away. Focus on the shape, colour and description given by the client to move it out of the body.
20. Move to your client's back and place your hands on their shoulders for a few moments, to gain rapport again. Look down through the crown chakra and see a ball of white light moving into the heart chakra. State a positive affirmation to yourself, three times. Intend the affirmation to be accepted by the subconscious mind. Try this: "You are now completely healed by Divine love and wisdom".
21. Place your dominant hand on the back of your client, over the heart chakra, and your other hand on their shoulder. Say to yourself "I now seal this process with divine love and wisdom", while picturing a door with CKR on it being closed and locked. Intend that the process is sealed and complete and that the client is healed.
22. Place your hands back on the client's shoulders and say to yourself "We are both blessed by this process". Imagine a shaft of brilliant white light shining down onto yourself and the student. Bathe in the light.
23. Move back so that you are facing your client, hold your hands at waist level with your palms facing your client, exhale, and release the Huiyin and tongue.
24. Ask the client to take a few long deep breaths and to come back slowly and open their eyes.
25. Ask if the shape is still there, and if so, if it has changed. If more needs to be done then use Psychic surgery or a Reiki treatment.

It is possible to carry out a healing attunement remotely, through the use of the distant healing symbol and your imagination, or a suitable prop like a teddy bear.

Tatsumi's Ritual

Introduction

Tatsumi was Hayashi's last Master before Hawayo Takata, and he was discovered by Dave King (no relation) of the Traditional Japanese Reiki Association in Canada. Dave saw Tatsumi's notes, which he had copied out by hand as part of his training with Dr Hayashi, and witnessed some sort of an attunement ritual. What is described below, then, is **perhaps** similar to the attunement procedure that Dr Hayashi used, and presumably he taught this method to Mrs Takata also... so **maybe** this is how the Western attunement styles started.

But there is some disagreement now in the world of Reiki about whether this ritual is actually an 'attunement' or whether it is a ritual that acknowledges someone's advancement to a particular stage of development, but in any case it is interesting to see a ritual that Tatsumi seems to have been taught by Dr Hayashi and I am not suggesting that you use this ritual in practice. I am including it in this manual for information only.

Preparation

The student is seated on a chair with back straight and with (stockinged) feet flat on the floor. Use a cushion if necessary to get correct elevation of feet. The student's hands are placed in prayer position and their eyes are closed. Use the attunement music and make sure that the student is grounded.

First Degree

Stand behind the student, draw the Master Symbol in the air and move it over your own body.

Clear the student's energy by making three descending sweeps of the hands from above the student's head to the ground.

1. Place your non-dominant hand on (or just above) the student's crown chakra and place your dominant hand just above it.

2. Draw the symbols in order - #1, #2, #3, #4 with the dominant hand over the crown. As you do so focus on opening the Reiki channels.

3. Place your hands on the student's shoulders for a few seconds with the intent of grounding.

4. Stand in front of the student and open the student's hands.

5. Place your dominant hand slightly above the student's hands and your other hand slightly below the student's hands. Focus on opening the Reiki channels and hold the position until you feel a good energy flow.

6. Place the student's hands back into the prayer position and blow gently and continuously along the space between the hands going from thumb side palm to little finger side palm. Rotate the student's hands whilst doing this.

7. Give a short, sharp blast of breath to the student's crown chakra, heart chakra and dan-tien chakra (just below navel).

8. Go behind the student and make a single upward sweep from floor to above student's head. Bow.

9. Take the student's right hand and place it on the student's left shoulder. Take the student's left hand and place it on the student's right shoulder.

10. Place your hands on the student's shoulders and `revive' student. Ask about experiences etc.

Second Degree/Master levels

Stand behind the student, draw the Master Symbol in the air and move it over your own body.

Clear the student's energy by making three descending sweeps of the hands from above the student's head to the ground.

1. Place your non-dominant hand on (or just above) the student's crown chakra and place your dominant hand just above it.

2. Draw the symbols in order - #1, #2, #3, #4 with the dominant hand over the crown. As you do so focus on the symbol that you are attuning.

3. Place your hands on the student's shoulders for a few seconds with the intent of grounding.

4. Stand in front of the student and open the student's hands.

5. Place your dominant hand slightly above the student's hands and your other hand slightly below the student's hands. Draw the appropriate symbol four times with the upper hand then `lead' the symbol into the student's palm.

6. Place the student's hands back into the prayer position and blow gently and continuously along the space between the hands going from thumb side palm to little finger side palm. Rotate the student's hands whilst doing this.

7. Give a short, sharp blast of breath to the student's crown chakra, heart chakra and dan-tien chakra (just below navel).

8. Go behind the student and make a single upward sweep from floor to above student's head. Bow.

9. Take the student's right hand and place it on the student's left shoulder. Take the student's left hand and place it on the student's right shoulder.

10. Place your hands on the student's shoulders and `revive' student. Ask about experiences etc.

Differences

At Point 2, in the first degree attunement you use all four symbols with the intention that you are opening the channels. At second degree and Master levels you use all four symbols again, but you focus on the symbol that you are attuning to on that occasion (there are three different attunements at Second Degree level and one attunement at Master level).

At Point 5, in the first degree attunement you hold your hands on either side of the student's hands with the intention of opening the Reiki channels. At second degree and Master levels you draw the Reiki symbol you are attuning to on that occasion four times and lead it into the palm.

Japanese Empowerments

 Master Course Audio CD Number 1 - track #9

Background

In Autumn 1999 something new arrived in the world of Western Reiki: Reiju empowerments. They were introduced to the world by a man called Hiroshi Doi who was/is a member of the Usui Reiki Ryoho Gakkai, the Usui Memorial Society. Mr Doi's Reiju was a reconstruction of the empowerments used in the memorial society, which he had not been taught to carry out because he had not achieved Master level within the 'Gakkai. So in the same way that the Imperial Officers had put together attunements as a constructed ritual that gave them the same sort of experience that they had when they were being empowered by Mikao Usui, Mr Doi put together his 'Reiju' as a way of reproducing his experiences when being empowered during his 'Gakkai training.

Mr. Doi, a student of former Gakkai president Mrs. Kimiko Koyama, explained that in the Usui Reiki Ryoho Gakkai, students attend weekly training sessions called "Shuyokai" where they practise "Hatsurei ho". After the last step of Hatsurei ho, in Seishin Toitsu (concentration), students would meditate for a while. That is when the teachers would give Reiju to each one of the students in meditation. Through these training sessions and their own practices, the students' Reiki channelling power (or ability) would advance.

Interestingly, Mr Doi's 'reconstructed' Reiju is similar to the "Reiju" ritual used by Usui Sensei's surviving students, a Tendai Buddhist blessing ritual which came to the West via their contact Chris Marsh.

Most people within the world of Reiki who are using Reiju empowerments will be using Mr Doi's reconstructed Reiju, since this ritual has been taught every year since Autumn 1999 at various "URRI" gatherings in different parts of the world, and then passed on to other teachers by the people who attended these courses. "URRI" stands for "Usui Reiki Ryoho International" and is the banner under which Mr Doi's courses were presented. There have been annual URRI gatherings in Canada, Japan, Spain and Denmark, though the 2003 gathering in Denmark was the last.

But we should not focus our attention too much on the 'Gakkai and their practices, such as we know what they are, because the 'Gakkai was set up after Usui Sensei's death by the Imperial Officers, who had been taught a system that was not representative of what Usui had been teaching to all the other students, they had not trained with Usui for very long and so were his least experienced Master students, and after the 'Gakkai was established they changed things wholesale even quite early on in its history.

The Reiju empowerments that you will be learning have come from Usui Sensei's surviving students, via Chris Marsh, though you will also understand how Mr Doi's reconstructed Reiju differs from the earlier form.

In the "attunements" section of this manual you will have read that recently one of Dr Hayashi's Master students – Mrs Yamaguchi – was discovered in Japan, and some Western Masters have taken training in her "Jikiden" Reiki with her and her son Tadao. Apparently she referred to the connection ritual she used as "Reiju", according to someone I spoke to who had trained with her. It seems to have been a fairly simple ritual, too, though, from what the student said, it was definitely not the same as the Reiju used by the surviving students, but may be similar to or a precursor of what Hayashi had taught to Mrs Takata.

Although you have learned to carry out Western attunements, you will probably choose in practice to use Reiju empowerments on any First and Second Degree courses that you might run, though a few of my Masters use a combination of attunements and empowerments on their courses. It is not necessary to use Western attunements at any stage of Reiki teaching: First Degree, Second Degree or Master level. Reiju empowerments are equivalent to attunements in terms of 'connecting' students to the energy, and they can be used instead of them at all levels. In fact, Reiju empowerments produce their own special benefits, and you can read more about that below.

Usui and the Origins of Reiju

Mikao Usui empowered his students regularly as part of their training at all levels. What he did can be referred to as "Reiju" – blessing of the five powers, a blessing made with the intention that the student should receive what they need. In order to achieve this, Mikao Usui used intent only, and students received their empowerments either in Usui Sensei's presence or as they left his presence. Usui did not use any physical ritual to achieve this: he used intent alone.

What was Usui doing? In essence he was transferring a Tendai Buddhist blessing, the sort of blessing that a Tendai teacher would bestow on his students, made with the intention that the student should receive what they need.

Within Tendai Buddhism there are two ways that this blessing can be carried out, two 'forms' of blessing: there was an 'internal' form and an 'external' form. The internal form of Reiju is what Mikao Usui used, using intention alone, and it seems only possible to use this method effectively if the teacher has progressed a great deal in terms of their spiritual development.

Within Tendai Buddhism, an 'external' form of Reiju is available for the benefit of teachers who have not yet developed sufficiently to be able to transfer the blessing effectively using intent alone, and the ritual ensures that the less-spiritually-developed teacher is still able to transfer what was intended, by using a set of formal movements, an external ritual, which is what you will be learning shortly.

The Reiju that you will be learning is used routinely by Usui Sensei's surviving students as a teaching tool; it is a way of enabling less spiritually advanced students to transfer the blessing effectively, and it represents the essence of what Mikao Usui was transferring using intent alone.

You can write "Reiju" in two different ways using Japanese kanji, one way means "accepting the spirituality" and the other means "giving the spirituality". The word Reiju has also been translated as the 'giving of the five blessings', or 'the five powers'. The five powers are 'given' by each of the five hand positions/points that are held after the crown has been opened (see Reiju instructions below). The five powers allow the student to develop fundamental qualities from which the Buddhist Way is cultivated:

1. The Power of Faith (Confidence)
2. The Power of Zeal (Energy, Effort)
3. The Power of Mindfulness
4. The Power of Meditation
5. The Power of Wisdom

Reiju is a 'spiritual empowerment', it is not just a mini-attunement: it is much more than that:

1. Reiju 'connects' the student to Reiki and continually reinforces that connection, increasing the strength of the student's Reiki. The student can work on and develop that enhanced connection by practising Hatsurei ho daily.

2. Reiju enhances the student's spiritual development and self-healing, moving the student along his/her spiritual path. This aspect is enhanced through Hatsurei ho and, for example, meditating on the energies introduced at Second Degree level, and carrying our regular self-empowerments at Master level.

3. Receiving Reiju empowerments on a regular basis is the key to maximising intuition, and, in the 'Gakkai, students work on and develop this potential by practising Reiji ho. The surviving students seemed to have had no problem in working intuitively.

Below you are going to learn how to perform the Reiju sequence, the physical movements of which are the same at all Reiki levels (First Degree, Second Degree, Master level).

Then we will move on to discover how Reiju is used in practice at First Degree, Second Degree and Master levels, because something slightly different is done in your head at the different levels.

Giving Reiju

 Master Course Audio CD Number 2 - track #1

 DVD Video sequence

Reiju empowerments consist of two stages:

1. A general introductory stage where you open yourself to the energy and create sacred space. This is done only once, at the start of the Reiju session, no matter how many students you will be empowering.

2. The individual empowerments for each student.

Introductory Stage

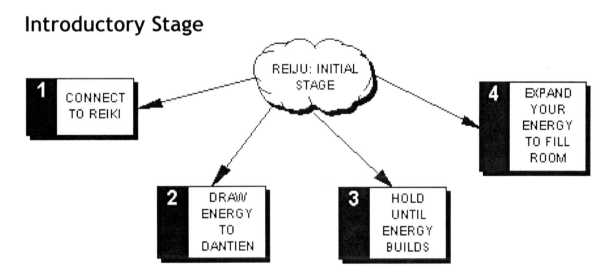

The Introductory stage of Reiju is described below. This is a reconstruction that has come to us from Hiroshi Doi. The surviving students do carry out a ritual to prepare themselves and the room before performing Reiju, but details of this ritual are not available, so we will use Mr Doi's ritual, and it works very well in practice.

You will be making one movement that opens you up to Reiki and brings Reiki into your Tanden (Dantien, Hara). Then you will be making three repeated movements that expand your energy to include or engulf the people who are going to receive Reiju from you, expanding your energy to fill the room, connecting you to them and creating sacred space.

144

1. Raise hands to connect to Reiki in the way that you learned as part of Hatsurei ho.

2. Feel energy or light cascading down into your hands, through your arms and into your Tanden.

3. Bring your hands slowly out to the sides, imagining that as you do this you are bringing energy through your crown, flooding the energy over your body and passing this energy through your body to your Tanden point as you lower your hands. Finish this movement by hovering your hands in front of your Tanden, with the dominant hand closest, and the non-dominant hand hovering further away.

4. You have now surrounded yourself with energy and brought the energy into your Tanden.

5. Hold this position until you feel a real sense of connectedness with the energy. Maybe you can feel a strong bolt of energy through your crown, your hands may heat up or fill with energy, or you may feel changes in your Tanden.

6. This movement is done only once, and we follow this with three repeated movements...

7. Move your hands away from your Tanden, straight out in front of you, moving your hands forwards and upwards to above your head, to achieve the same 'connecting position' that you learned in Hatsurei ho.

8. Bring your hands slowly out to the sides, just like before, this time imagining that as you do so you are expanding your energy to engulf the people you will be empowering.

9. Return your hands to your Tanden point as before.

10. Repeat this 'expanding' sequence two more times, each time finishing with your hands hovering in front of your Tanden.

This introductory sequence is based on the teachings of Hiroshi Doi. While the surviving students did carry out some sort of 'opening' or introductory ritual or sequence, this is not available to us. The sequence Mr Doi uses works very well.

The sequence seems to be the reverse of something called Shaou Gong, a closing down exercise used at the end of a QiGong session, so the above can be seen as opening up the person to energy. It also seems to be similar to a QiGong exercise called Parting the Clouds.

NOTE: This Introductory stage can be used out of context in these situations:

1. As part of Western-style Reiki Attunements
2. Before you are about to start Reiki treatments

Reiju Empowerments: introductory stage

First Movement:
Connect to Reiki

Move your hands down to the sides, exhaling. As you do this, draw energy down through your crown.

The energy flows down the centre of your body.

Flowing towards your Tanden

Hold hands in front of Tanden until strongly connected to the energy

Then start three repeated movements: hands go forwards

Outwards & upwards, back to the 'connecting' position

Get ready for the three movements...

Now you are going to bring your hands down to the sides, and then along to the Tanden, exhaling as you do so, returning your hands to the connecting position (forwards, outwards & upwards) in between each downwards movement.

With each downward movement you 'expand' your energy to engulf the people who will be receiving Reiju from you. Flood the room with energy, with light.

Individual Empowerments

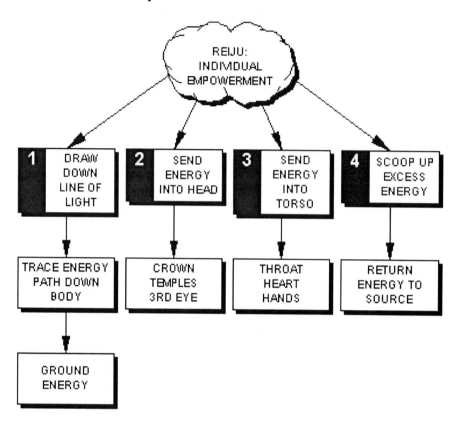

The recipient should sit on a chair, relaxed, holding their hands in the Gassho position and with their eyes closed. Although Reiju empowerments are usually given as part of the Hatsurei ho sequence at the Gakkai's weekly training sessions, the empowerments can also be given on their own, without Hatsurei ho being practised by the recipient.

1. Stand in front of the recipient. In Japan they would do Gassho and bow one time.

2. Touch the recipient's shoulder to indicate that they should place their hands in Gassho, if they are not already doing the meditation that follows the Seishin Toitsu stage of Hatsurei ho.

3. Move your hands high up above you, with your fingers splayed, and feel energy coming down into your hands from above.

4. **ENERGY PATH:** Move your hands down a little and join together the first two joints of your index fingers, with the other fingers floppy and relaxed.

5. In one continuous movement, move your hands down in front of the recipient, and draw down a line of light which enters the crown, and trace an energy path down the centre of the body, intending that you are opening the energy centres as you do so. Keep on tracing the energy path until you are pointing at the base of the spine, at which time your hands will be close to the recipient's knees.

147

6. Part your hands and, with your palms face down, move your hands sideways past the knees and move them downwards towards the floor, ritually grounding the energy without touching the floor. Move your hands to the sides as you stand up straight.

7. Now you are going to be holding a number of hand positions where you will be flooding an area with light or energy. Each position should be held for a count of at least ten seconds.

8. **CROWN:** Stand up and move your hands down so that they are hovering, one over another, above the recipient's crown. If the recipient has long legs, you may want to stand to one side of them, so you do not have to lean forwards uncomfortably. Touch the recipient's aura above their head using your dominant hand, and hover your non-dominant hand over your dominant hand, palms face down. Direct energy down the energy path that you traced with the previous hand movement. Hiroshi Doi believes that this stage helps to 'clarify the energy body' and attune the energy body with the cosmic rhythm.

9. **TEMPLES:** Following the outline of the aura, move your hands to both sides of the recipient's head. Each palm faces the side of the recipient 's head (at about the height of the eyebrows). Hiroshi Doi believes that you are expanding the energy path so that the student's entire body is being flooded with Reiki.

10. **THIRD EYE:** Again following the outline of the aura, move your hands to the front of the recipient's face and make a triangle with your index finger and thumb tips, with the other fingers splayed out. This is said to be the symbol of the sun. Hold the centre of the triangle in front of the recipient's third eye. Your palms are facing their face. Hiroshi Doi believes that you are flooding the third eye with light, and this is said to help the third eye to function more sensitively and to connect with higher-level consciousness.

11. **THROAT:** This is an intermediate step that does not come from Hiroshi Doi, but through some contacts closer to Usui. Hold the hands behind, and in front of, the throat, and flood the throat with light.

12. **HEART:** This is an intermediate step that does not come from Hiroshi Doi, but through some contacts closer to Usui. Hold the hands behind, and in front of, the heart area, and flood the heart with light. If you cannot place your hand in between the hands and the heart, simply direct Reiki into the heart with your palm outside the hands.

13. **HANDS:** Touching together the tips of your first three fingers, move your hands down and around the recipient's hands, without touching their hands. Let energy flow through the recipient's hands: flood the hands with light. Hiroshi Doi believes that the intention here is to connect "the centre of the student" and "the centre of the universe", create an 'energy path' from the shoulders to the arms, from the arms to the palms, and to integrate left energy and right energy.

14. Move your hands up and over the recipient's fingertips, and bring your hands down towards the knees (your three fingertips are still touching at this stage). Smoothly

separate your hands and, with your palms face down, move your hands sideways past the knees and curve them round in a circle towards the floor.

15. With the intention that you are 'scooping up' excess energy and returning it to the source of Reiki, bring your hands together. Your palms face upwards, making contact with the tips of the two smallest fingers of each hand, and with the side of your palms touching along their length also - rather as if you were scooping up water from a stream. Move your hands up, pointing your fingers towards the centre of the recipient's body as if you were scooping up the energy and returning it to the sky, returning the energy along the energy path that you traced earlier. As your hands reach towards the sky, open your arms, releasing the little finger contact toward the end of the movement.

16. In Japan they would do Gassho and bow.

This sequence is as taught by Usui Sensei's surviving students, as passed on by Chris Marsh.

In Hiroshi Doi's version of Reiju the "Throat" and "Heart" stages are not included, so you would go straight from the forehead to the hands.

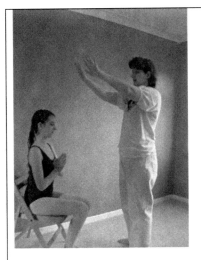

Connect to energy with fingers splayed

Join together first two index finger joints

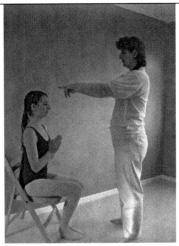

Draw down a line of light that enters the crown

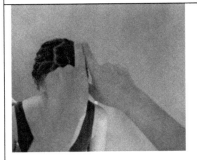

Hand position illustrated in more detail

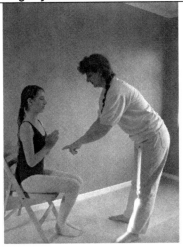

Trace energy path down centre

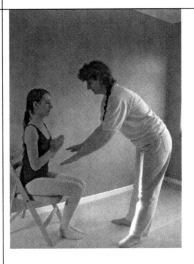

Part hands over the knees

Move palms towards ground

Ground the energy without touching the ground

Move hands out to the sides

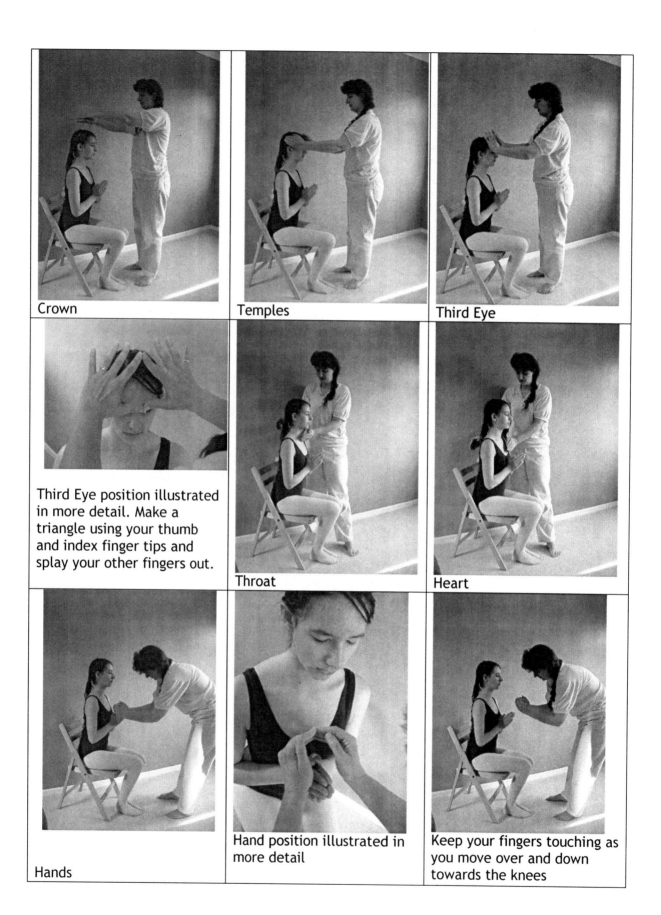

Crown

Temples

Third Eye

Third Eye position illustrated in more detail. Make a triangle using your thumb and index finger tips and splay your other fingers out.

Throat

Heart

Hands

Hand position illustrated in more detail

Keep your fingers touching as you move over and down towards the knees

151

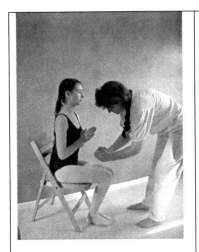

Now you can part your hands

Move your hands scooping round in a circle

Bring your hands together at the bottom of the circle

Join together the side of your palm and the tips of your two smallest fingers

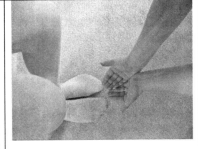

The hand position is illustrated here. You are scooping up any excess energy and you are going to return it back to the source...

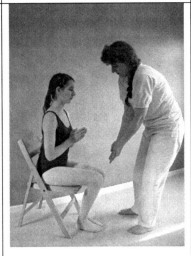

Return

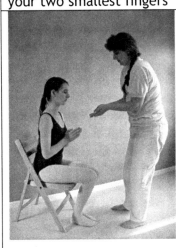

To

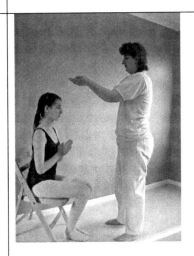

The

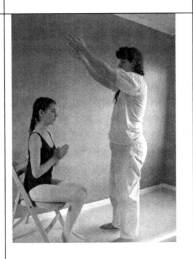

Source

First Degree Empowerments

The Reiju empowerments that you have read about above can be used as an alternative to Reiki First Degree attunements. Carry out the empowerment with the intention that the recipient is permanently connected to Reiki, that they should receive what they need.

How many you perform during your course is down to your personal preference. It is nice to do a few; I do three because it fits in nicely with my schedule. Ideally, people would then have access to regular Reiju, because this helps to enhance intuition and spiritual development. This could be in person or at a distance.

Second Degree Empowerments

We should not be surprised that Usui did not have one standard way of connecting his students to the energies and moving them from one level to another. What he did with them depended on their background.

'Buddhist approach'

One way of dealing with things was to carry out plain Reiju at all levels. At Reiki1 and Reiki2 levels the intention was that the recipient should receive what they needed. Alongside this, the student would carry out the various meditations that were designed to enhance their awareness of their hara (a preparation for second-degree), and at second-degree level allowed them to fully experience earth energy, heavenly energy, and oneness... the 'Buddhist' meditation approach. The Buddhist-style meditations used to experience earth ki and heavenly ki etc. can be found in the 'meditations' section of this manual. Once they student had fully assimilated the energy, they would have been the corresponding kotodama to use.

'Shinto approach'

But this was not the only approach, and one of Usui students – who followed Shinto – carried out empowerments in conjunction with the Reiki kotodama. This is how it was done...

At second-degree, there would be three empowerments, one empowerment representing each of the three energies/states that are taught at Second Degree level. While carrying out each empowerment, you would intone the kotodama silently to yourself, either three times for each hand position, or endlessly as you go through the sequence from crown to hands. This has the effect of giving the empowerment the 'flavour' of that energy, flooding the recipient with one aspect of the energy during each separate empowerment.

Reiju #1	intone the 'focus' Kotodama.
Reiju #2	intone the 'harmony' Kotodama.
Reiju #3	intone the 'connection' Kotodama.

These empowerments have the effect of connecting you to, or emphasising to you, or 'flagging up to you', the essence of the energies associated with the Reiki kotodama. This gives each empowerment a distinctive 'flavour', and some people can actually tell which empowerment they have received, or certainly they notice that the empowerment produces within them feelings that echo the experiences they have when either meditating on the Reiki symbols or experiencing the energies of the kotodama.

Once these empowerments had been given, the students would use regular chanting of the Kotodama in order to learn to become earth Ki, to become heavenly Ki, and to experience oneness. They would focus on one aspect of the energy at a time for many months before moving on to the next, so for example a student would spend 6-9 months meditating on earth ki before moving on to spend a similar period meditating on heavenly ki.

Where does that leave the Reiki symbols?

Despite the fact that one is not 'attuned to the symbols' by the above process, the Reiki symbols work for students connected using Reiju in the same way as if they had been 'attuned' to the symbols in the Western tradition. In fact, the symbols will work for a student even at First Degree level using 'plain' Reiju (with no symbols entering into the process, of course).

It seems that the widely held Western view that the symbols are useless unless you are specifically attuned to them is incorrect. If you are attuned to Reiki then the symbols represent the energy in much the same way that the Kotodama represent the energy, but Reiki is the energy, not the symbols, and once you are connected to Reiki then **any** symbol will push the energy in a particular direction.

Master Level Empowerments

Again, Usui had different approaches. We have already seen that at Reiki1 and Reiki2 levels you might have used just 'plain' Reiju with the intention that the recipient should receive what they needed. Students carried out various meditations to experience the second-degree energies/states. The alternative was to carry out empowerments that flooded the student with the essence of the three kotodama: one empowerment was used for each of the three second-degree kotodama, and then students used kotodama to learn to 'become' those energies and that state.

Well at Master level there were a couple of choices too. You could carry out plain Reiju, but with a different intention: you intended that the recipient "be enabled to learn to transfer energy" (the ability).

The Shinto, or Kotodama, version of this would have been to carry out the empowerment while intoning the 'empowerment' Kotodama. While carrying out the empowerment, you would intone the empowerment kotodama silently to yourself, either three times for each hand position, or endlessly as you go through the sequence from the crown to the hands. This has the effect of giving the empowerment the 'flavour' of that energy, flooding the recipient with that energy during the empowerment.

This is the approach that I recommend.

The Benefits of Reiju Empowerments

I have had the opportunity to compare the experiences of students connected to Reiki using Western-style attunements, and Reiju empowerments. In my experience "Reiju" students seem better connected to the energy right from the start, more sensitive to the energy and better able to work intuitively. It seems to do something really special for them.

I have seen Reiju discussed on Internet discussion groups in the past, and the general consensus that I saw was that other teachers had come to the same conclusion: that Reiju was doing something very special for students. There was one dissenting voice, someone who did not notice any difference in their students' reactions, but everyone else who commented felt that Reiju 'worked better' in some way.

One of my "Original Usui Reiki" students a few years ago sent me an e-mail to say that she had started using Reiju on her Reiki courses instead of Western attunements and that her Reiju students were "flying" when compared to her students who had been connected using attunements.

Western Reiju Variations

I know a Reiki Master who - before we had learned about the kotodama - used Reiju three times at Reiki1 level, one Reiju for each of the three symbols. For Reiju #1 he visualised CKR passing into the third eye while holding the 'triangle' there, for Reiju #2 he visualised SHK in the same place, and for Reiju #3 he visualised HSZSN there. This seems to have worked fine.

This Master had also used Reiju empowerments with symbols at Reiki2 level. This time he again did three Reiju empowerments, one for each symbol. For Reiju #1 he visualised CKR passing into the third eye (as before) and visualised CKR passing into the hands while he cupped his own hands around them. For Reiju #2 he used SHK in this way, and in Reiju #3 he used HSZSN. Again, he says that this worked well.

He has also used Reiju at Master level, with impressive results seemingly, sending DKM into the third eye and hands. Again, this was before we knew about the kotodama.

He has tried giving people Reiju without physically doing anything to them, by simply intending that the recipients would receive the empowerment, or the empowerment energy. He says that this works powerfully too, and we will talk more about this below.

Students' Experiences

In this section you can read the experiences of some of our 'home study course' students in different parts of the world, talking about their work with Reiju empowerments. Maybe your experiences will echo theirs, maybe your experiences will be quite different.

"I feel quite excited at the moment, I have practised the Reiju exercises as you direct over the last two weeks. I can only say that I feel inspired, and yet humbled by the whole experience of learning with you. The Reiju empowerments are very touching and bring together the complete essence of energy and people. The person I worked with over the last few weeks has really been enthused also. This has been so much more in a profound way than the experience I had at first and even second degree with others.

"I carried out this exercise on my sister Jean. On beginning this Reiju empowerment I myself felt the energy - not just a heat or tingling in my hands - but the actual energy - especially over her crown chakra. I personally felt connected and intune with the vibrations of the energy and saw it as a pure form of initiating Reiki. It is similar to the Great Tai-Chi circle ritual which expands, connects and focuses chi awareness. Jean felt a lot of energy over the left side of her brain. She felt that Reiju is less cluttered and a smoother process, and as a recipient she felt the energy more. She said that it was less ritualistic, more a simpler and nicer way - with the movements of Reiju connecting to the energy in a way that Western attunements don"t."

"Well, I've just had the best time so far on my course this week!! WOW!! I LOVE the Reiju empowerments!!! After the 'mechanical' process of the attunements, working with the Reiju empowerments has been like dancing :o) (...dancing and music are 'in my blood', so for me that is an apt description, the movements were the dance and Reiki was the music!) They flow so smoothly! I only watched the video twice, then listened to the audio track, then I actually went through an empowerment using the audio track....and WOW, I felt the energy flowing immediately! I felt comfortable from my first 'attempt', and have had no problem remembering the whole 'sequence' since then, so I feel so much more confident with the empowerments and I now have a very well empowered prop!

"While 'sending/doing' and empowerment, I feel a huge flow of Reiki. I find that the energy builds very quickly once I have connected at the beginning, and expanding to 'engulf' the recipient almost happens automatically while I'm following the sequence of movements. While 'bringing' the energy down into the crown of the recipient, I can 'see' white light flowing into the crown chakra, and moving down through the chakras. I also can feel a 'beam' of energy flowing through me, and out from my fingers along the line I am 'drawing' the energy down. I was amazed the first time it happened!!...in my minds eye there was this bright white triangle of energy flowing into my prop, and through me, from the source!!! :o) While 'putting' the energy in at the third eye, I can 'see' white triangles of light going from my hands and entering the chakra and getting smaller as they 'go deeper'. I often feel these pulsing more than flowing, as one reaches the chakra, the next one 'leaves my hands'.

"While using each of the level 2 and the empowerment kotodama, I have the same strong feel of the individual energy 'sending' that I have while receiving the empowerments. In fact, as it's been rather warm this week, I found using the focus kotodama rather uncomfortable, I was so hot!! So I've only 'used' that one a couple of times!! I've preferred the more 'cooling' energy of the Harmony kotodama for practice! One thing I've really noticed this week, is the increase in the intensity of each energy, it's as though it's 'kicked up a notch' since I began doing the empowerments... [and I love the fact that I can now decide which one I would like to experience any time I like :o)] I'm using the empowerment kotodama for all my self-empowerments each morning, so I enjoy using the others to send myself a distant one, 'variety is the spice of life' they say...

"The other big difference with the empowerments (compared to the attunements) is that I already feel involved, instead of just feeling I'm going through the motions of the attunements and not 'feeling' what I'm doing :o) I've thoroughly enjoyed this week :o) And I'll probably find lots of excuses to practice on myself for a long time yet!"

Distant Connections

The first thing to say about distant attunements, or distant Reiju empowerments, is that they work. I have had experience of carrying out both of these for many years, and a distant Master attunement that I carried out in August 2000 gave me one of the most powerful experiences that I have had. Someone said to me recently that 'all attunements are distant attunements', emphasising to us that it is not the Reiki Master who attunes someone, any more than it is the practitioner who heals... the Reiki Master is just the channel, the vehicle through which the attunement comes, the catalyst, the mediator, and not the origin of the attunement. The attunement comes from above; we just make the introductions between the recipient and the source, and we can make the introductions standing in front of the student or 1,000 miles away.

Distant Reiju

It is perfectly possible to arrange for another Reiki Master to send you distant Reiju. When I have done this, I have had an empty chair in front of me and imagined that the person I am sending the empowerment to is in front of me. Alternatively, when carrying out the 'self-empowerment' stage of Reiju (see above) I have imagined my energy expanding to engulf the other person at their home.

When Reiju first arrived in the West, a few of us got together to do distant Reiju on each other to see what would happen. Every Sunday evening we would sit down and, at our allotted time, we would send Reiju to the other two people. I would go through the movements on an imaginary person (people) in front of me.

When I was receiving, at the allotted time I felt my head fill up with flickering white light, and then purple lights, after a while my third eye started fizzing and pulsing, and a little later my hands heated up and tingled like crazy. The sensations stopped at the exact time that the sender stopped sending the empowerment (we swapped notes shortly afterwards).

I have used distant Reiju to attune someone who was not attuned previously - the daughter of a friend of mine. Immediately after the distant Reiju empowerment the little girl was able to channel Reiki. She was not consciously aware of the empowerment because she was distracted doing other things rather than sitting expectantly.

We should not be too surprised that this works, because we do not actually attune someone, we are just essential bystanders... making the introductions, so to speak.

I send a Reiju 'broadcast' every Monday, with the intention that it be received by anyone who wishes to 'tune in' to it any time that day. People have felt it all over the world. Here are some messages that I received from people in various parts of the globe, in response to my distant empowerments:

158

... at 9:00pm waves of energy washed over me. Hardly any vibrating, just a light, fizzy energy. My hands and feet were full of Reiki.
Essex

I sat down a little before 9.15pm cleared my mind.... there was a wonderful feeling of being light and a faint buzzing around my head, then gentle pressure on my crown....plenty of warmth followed. As things progressed I could sense movement around me. It was as if you were standing in front of me...had the impression of gentle swaying...for a moment the room was light. I felt a need to put my hands in the prayer position...felt movement and warmth, with some tingling. Don't remember putting my hands down, but I did!!
Hertfordshire

I felt very peaceful and could feel the energy coming from the front, my crown was filled with the energy expanding , then as if you were standing in front of me , the various positions with energy softly expanding. The third eye was throbbing and continued to do so after I felt the transmission was completed. I thought I had been sat for ages, when I felt the process was complete, I thanked the Reiki Guides and realised it had only been 10 minutes from my sitting to completion.
Australia

I went up to bed at 8.45pm and laid down, I felt really warm and fuzzy and went out like a light!!!
Wiltshire

I am going thru' quite a sad time right now and I can feel that this reiju empowerment has given me the courage and strength I need to assist and empower me to walk peacefully thru' this part of my journey. I could see the shimmering light come down into my crown and spread throughout my whole being, "telling me that all is well, we are with you always dearest one". Today, there has been a lot of tears and releasing and I "know" that I am being guided out of this mist of despair.
Scotland

After a few minutes I felt A great deal of energy, followed by a strong feeling of heat in my solar plexus and then my heart chakra. I then saw waves of purple and greeny gold coming towards me and breaking over me, my fingers were tingling the whole time, and then it all suddenly stopped.
Essex

"I've been able to send several distant 'simple' empowerments to a Reiki 1 attuned friend too. I felt a little nervous sending the first one, so I asked for 'guidance' through it (security!), and held the intention that she would receive what she needed to from the empowerment (as she is already connected it seemed a more appropriate intention at the time). She hadn't felt anything during her Reiki 1 attunements, so I was very pleasantly surprised and pleased….(OK!!…OVER THE MOON!!) when she had some positive feedback for me, right from the first one :o). She felt energy entering her crown, it appeared to pulse (heavier and lighter was her description), and she felt 'pressure' around her third eye, throat and heart area. The most noticeable feeling for her though, was the 'ball of energy' that she felt building between her hands throughout the empowerment, which became larger each time, and she said that her hands began to part to 'accommodate' the size of it :o) I found it very straightforward connecting to her to send the empowerment. I found that I could either 'be' with her, or imagine her in the chair, either method worked. I felt a large flow of energy while sending the empowerments. And 'coincidentally' I also felt that the energy pulsed, especially at the crown area. After the first one, I felt a lot more confident, and although I still 'asked for guidance' I didn't feel that I needed it to 'get me through', but more as an extra helping hand :o) I actually didn't feel that she was at a distance at all for any of them. And I experienced all the same 'things' that I felt while practising on myself and my prop, but more intensely in many ways, because I was 'interacting' directly with another person :o) I always see colours while I'm 'working' with Reiki, and throughout all of the empowerments I've done, I've been seeing a wonderful array of all colours, not just the ones that I usually see for each energy!"

Distant Attunements

In August 2000 I carried out a distant Master attunement on a friend of mine - someone who is already a Reiki Master. I performed the attunement on an imaginary person sitting in front of me on an empty swivel chair, and started by intending a strong connection between myself and the recipient. I went through the attunement as normal, sending the symbols, tapping and blowing etc, intending that the recipient was in front of me rather than being 300 miles away.

From the moment I started I felt amazingly charged with energy, and rather than being a mechanical process it became a wonderful flowing exchange of energy, and I felt merged with the energy and the recipient so strongly; it was an astonishing experience. The whole process took just seven minutes. It was a very powerful experience for the recipient too.

'Intention Attunements'

We can even push this further, and carry out 'intention' attunements or empowerments, where we do not even imagine any particular ritual, or stages, or hand positions. Simply connect with the other person and intend that they receive an attunement or empowerment, and just let the energy flow, with an empty head.

Here is some feedback I obtained from some of my Masters whom I experimented on...

Hi Taggart,

I sat in the garden and did the Gassho meditation today, just after 5pm, and linked into your empowerment.

I immediately felt energy on my face, as I do when Spirit draws close, and then the Crown Chakra became very active - a beautiful golden light spinning around the top of my head. The Crown stayed active throughout the remainder of the meditation.

Next, the energy focussed on the sides of my head and I noticed it around my ears. The Gold turned to daffodil yellow, then purple, then magenta.

The energy stayed there for some time and then shifted to the Third Eye, where I saw the colour purple and then indigo spinning clockwise.

Gradually the sensation of the energy disappeared and I opened my eyes and noticed that it was about 10 minutes from beginning to end.

Look forward to hearing what you've been doing this time :-)

Best wishes

Chris

Thanks, as ever, for the challenge.

I felt at first a strong wave of energy engulf me, like a warm, comforting blanket. Then the sensations seemed to localise themselves on my hands, and stay there for some time. Then I felt that blanketing again, and again the focus on the hands. Gradually, then, the energy diminished and I came out of reception.

Can't wait to hear what you've been up to!

Robert-Louis

Hi Taggart!

I received your empowerment about half an hour ago. It did feel quite different. It was generally more intense and the sensations were very dense. Normally I feel things going on in my crown and around the front of my face and my hands, tonight I felt tingling around the outer rim of the top of my head and lots of heat and heaviness in my fingers as time went on I felt an achy channel of energy running down from the top of my head to the base of my neck the energy felt like it was spiralling slowly sometimes it would seem to go anti clockwise and other times clockwise at this point my hands felt like they were one big heavy lump of energy and my fingers were burning and aching. Can't wait to find out what you did!

Best wishes

Tina

More Controversy

Sadly, there are people within the world of Reiki who are insisting that distant attunements do not, cannot and will not work. It seems strange to me that while these same people will be happy with the idea that distant healing can be sent from one side of the planet to another just by thinking about it, at the same time they will be arguing that attunements (or empowerments, for that matter) will only work if the teacher is corralled in the same room as the student. I wonder what the optimum distance between teacher and student is; maybe they think that attunements follow the 'inverse square law', just like gravity, where doubling the distance halves the potency. Who knows!

But you can't have it both ways: if distant healing works then distant attunements work. If distant attunements don't work then neither does distant healing, and no-one is seriously arguing this latter point.

We can look at this in a couple of ways. Firstly, many people see attunements as a way of 'connecting' the student to a new energy source that they were not connected to before – something 'external' to them - yet despite this they believe that the location of the teacher is a very important thing. This makes no sense: if you see empowerments (and attunements) as a way of 'making the introductions' between the student and the source of the energy, then attunements/empowerments are actually between the student and the source, not between the student and the teacher. The teacher is only the facilitator, and from this point of view all attunements or empowerments are in fact distant connections, because they are between the student and the source.

So, for people who believe that the connection is a way of hooking up the student to a new power source that is separate from the student, they are actually doing distant attunements all the time, and many of these people will claim that distant attunements do not work... yet they are in fact doing them themselves!

If you take the alternative view, where attunements/empowerments are a way of helping the student to recognise something that is already within them – a minority view which I subscribe to – then there is no 'distance' entering into the equation: the 'connection' is still between the student and that place within, and the teacher is a bystander, a facilitator. By this way of thinking, empowerments/attunements, whether carried out in the physical presence of the teacher or not, do not have any 'distance' to characterise them: the student is realising something that is already there within them.

There is a further point to make, actually, and it is this: some teachers like to think of themselves as being a powerful Reiki Master, they like the term Master and they like the idea that they can do things that other people apparently cannot. When giving attunements, they will see themselves as going in there to adjust the student's energy system, something that they know how to do because of their greater esoteric knowledge. The focus with these individuals is on themselves; they see themselves as being a very important part of the process, going in there and doing the ritual, waving their hands: **they** are doing the attunements. The idea of them not being centre stage in the process does not sit well with them. The important thing for them is their hands-on ability to manipulate and adjust, as they see it, to take control and be in charge, to be powerful, to be important and special.

So the idea that you can do this just as well 100 miles away using just your intention makes them feel less important, I believe. And of course if they have been taught that distant attunements do not work, and they are dogmatic and narrow minded, and unwilling to try things for themselves or open themselves to new ideas or new ways of working, the idea of distant attunements will be decidedly unsettling, and something that should be criticised and denigrated.

Self-Empowerments

There are various ways that people have found to give themselves empowerments.

Distant Reiju on yourself

You can, of course, do distant Reiju on yourself, with the intention that the empowerment will be received at whatever time you decide upon, or send it to be received whenever you sit down ready to receive it/ready to 'call it in'. Then sit yourself down with your hands in Gassho, at the appointed time if there is one, and receive the empowerment that you sent out earlier.

Using your 'Energy Body'

A variation of the distant Reiju that can be used on other people is to imagine you doing Reiju on yourself. Sit in a chair with your hands in Gassho, and imagine that you are standing in front of you. See yourself go through the self-empowerment stage, and then see yourself performing the empowerment on you.

Some people have tried sitting in a chair, and then they get up, imagining that they have left their 'energy body' or 'etheric double' behind in the chair. They then do the empowerment on their energy body. Other people have experimented using a mirror.

Self-Empowerments 'from the inside'

Reiki Master Carly Horbowiecz takes another approach. She simply visualises a line of light entering her crown and opening her energy centres down to the base of the spine, the energy then being grounded. Then she imagines, or rather feels or experiences, energy flowing through her crown down that energy path, then into her temples, then into her third eye and so on. So she experiences the energy's effects on herself, drawing the energy into the appropriate areas, without using the 'prop' of someone imagined outside her. She finds it very effective.

"Sending the distant empowerment to myself was rather strange. Going through the Reiju movements to send the empowerment - expanding the energy became almost hypnogogic - that stage between wakefulness and sleep - when on other occasions I have experienced an Alice in Wonderland sensation of growing bigger and bigger until it seems I and the universe are one. On receiving my own distant empowerment I felt tension around my head, like someone patting the air above me, and then stillness and silence and a drawing in. There was lots of iridescent purple. I felt an internal inward

connection to my inner self - very strange - lasting seconds only but I felt 'touched'.

"It was easy to see myself performing Reiju on myself - I could sense the movements and catch the shadow of these movements behind my closed eyelids. It was very meditative - seeing myself 'dancing the Tao' of the Reiju on myself. I felt the energy within and around me lifting - yes, empowering is the right word.
These exercises have been wonderful"

"I've tried all the methods of self-empowerment, on myself all week, I think the 'more traditional' way is my favourite, (though it's hard to decide as they are all so nice to 'use'), I've thoroughly enjoyed all the empowerments I've sent myself too (from both sides), and have tried all of the methods you describe :o) .... In fact I gave up using my prop by Tuesday and have 'practiced' by sending myself the empowerments since, visualising myself in the chair instead, then sitting down to 'receive' it :o)!! As you can imagine, I've been on rather a high all week!! I found the one 'method' described in the manual (Self-empowerments from the inside) very effective too. The 'energy' just exploded at each chakra :o) [In fact that's very close to a method I've used for years to 'reinforce' my connection with 'the source', which I learned years ago in an esoteric development group I belonged to! So when I initially read it I knew I would be able to use that method myself, so that was the first one I tried.] So I've found that all of the ways to send myself an empowerment, and also the different ways to do self-empowerments work wonderfully! :o)"

165

Meditations

Firstly, I would like to give a brief overview of the use of meditations with Usui Sensei's original system. Some of these you will already be familiar with, since they are included on my First and Second Degree courses. Some will be new to you. Paragraphs shown in **bold** are included later on in this section.

Overview of Usui's Meditations

 Master Course Audio CD Number 1 - track #11

First Degree

1. Students carried out Kenyoku and Joshin Kokkyu Ho, and this developed in the 'Gakkai into 'Hatsurei ho'.

2. Students practised a self-treatment meditation

3. **Students practised mindfulness.**

4. **Before moving on to Second Degree level, students worked to develop their Hara (Tanden) using a specific exercise, and their progression depended upon working for some time with a 'Hara Defining Exercise'.**

Second Degree

1. Mindfulness was emphasised more at this level.

2. Some students used Kotodama in order to 'become' earth ki, heavenly ki, and in order to experience a state of oneness. See earlier in this manual.

3. **Some students used Buddhist-style meditations in order to 'become' earth ki, heavenly ki, and in order to experience a state of oneness.**

4. **Prior to starting Master training, students learned to blend earth ki and heavenly ki within them.**

Master Level

1. Master students carried out a simple self-empowerment technique, using the empowerment kotodama, a technique that can be easily appended onto Hatsurei or Kenyoku/Joshin Kokkyu Ho. This would have been carried out regularly for an extended period of time before the student moved on.

2. Students developed this meditation further. The expanded meditation would have again been carried out for an extended period.

3. Then the student would move on to add a further meditation called 'sitting in Stupa', which eventually they would carry out on its own, leaving the earlier meditations behind.

4. Although some students never progressed beyond the 'sitting in stupa' stage, some moved on to meditate on Buddhist mandalas: the Womb mandala and the Diamond mandala.

5. A further mandala was introduced.

6. Only once these stages had been completed would the student be taught how to teach and empower others.

7. The final 'level' was left open, for the student to develop as far as they could.

Mindfulness

The concept of mindfulness was introduced to Usui's students at first-degree level, and that this concept was emphasised more at second-degree. In order to explain what mindfulness is, I have included a passage below which was given to me by Chris Marsh. For further information about mindfulness, which is really beyond the scope of this manual, you can search for this term on the Internet, and there are many books written on this subject. Here are two books that I can recommend:

The Miracle of Mindfulness
Thich Nhat Hanh, Rider, London

Peace is Every Step – a guide to mindfulness in everyday life
Thich Nhat Hanh, Rider, London

Mindfulness in Plain English
Bhante Henepola Gunaratana
Wisdom Publications, Boston

Some people also recommend this book:

The Power of Now
Eckhart Tolle
Hodder and Stoughton

Here is what Chris sent to me:

"Learning to live in the moment is a great and powerful skill that will help us in everything we do. To "be here now," relaxed and engaged in whatever we are doing, is to be alive and healthy. In Buddhism, the awareness of what is happening right now is called mindfulness.

In everyday life, mindfulness is an alert mind that is aware of every aspect that is going on, and what to do, without being scattered. In meditation, mindfulness is giving ourselves completely to our breathing, or whatever the exercise is.

Mindfulness is giving full attention to the present, without worries about the past or future. So often, we borrow trouble from the future by constantly thinking about what might befall us tomorrow, instead of dealing with one day at a time.

In Buddhism, the emphasis is on this very moment. We can guide our minds to live in the present, to do this we need to firmly establish a habit of total attention to what we are doing now. For every undertaking, we should consciously decide to keep other ideas, feelings, and activities out and give ourselves to what we are doing.

To be mindful doesn't mean to become emotionally intense or to stir up hosts of concepts in order to watch what we are thinking or doing. On the contrary, the mind is relaxed and calm, and therefore sharply aware of every event as it is, without conceptual and emotional struggle. However, when we notice that our mind is wandering, we should gently but firmly bring ourselves back to the present and to what we are doing. For most of us, especially in the beginning, we may need to do this again and again.

By remaining in a relaxed and spacious mood, we can live in a spontaneous stream of mindfulness and awareness. Our minds will become steadier, instead of constantly fragmenting into scattered thoughts and wildly chasing the past or future. After a while, our concentration will improve and we will find it easier to meditate. Learning how to enjoy and be in the present moment leads to openness and timeless time. By being mindful, we find the peace within ourselves.

The Hara Defining Exercise

Why would you want to define your hara?

In Japanese terms, the belly or abdomen, between the pubic bone and the rib cage, is known as the Hara. The vital energy is concentrated in the Tanden in the centre of the Hara, found two fingerbreadths below the tummy button and 1/3 of the way into your body. In Japanese cosmology the energies of Heaven and Earth unite here to bring power, harmony and spontaneity to our actions. The Tanden is seen as the seat of the soul, the centre of your personal universe. It is the point from which all your focus and strength originates, and so is used as a seat of strength in martial arts and energy cultivation techniques. It is also the centre of our intuitive faculties, and so is focused upon when seeking inspiration while carrying out calligraphy or flower arranging. The Tanden is center of life. Drawing energy into your Tanden is drawing energy into the centre of your life and soul

Using the power of the Hara allows the practitioner to increase their intuition and the sensitivity in their hands. It allows us to empathise with the recipient but allow distance so we do not take on another's problems. Because of this, it is recommended that when you prepare to give Reiki you should first become aware of the Hara and the centred feeling that this gives. Joshin Kokkyu Ho is one way of getting in touch with the Tanden, and you may find with practice that you can feel the energy strongly there.

But there is an energy exercise that was used in the original form of Reiki, which focuses specifically on allowing you to define, or experience, your Tanden, to experience its precise location and dimensions. This was carried out because of its powerful self-healing effects.

Makoto No Kokyu - the breath of truth

This exercise is very important. There is in fact a Tendai branch of Shugendo in which this hara defining exercise is the **only** self-healing exercise used, and is seen as the single most effective method to achieve self-healing. This has persisted within Shugendo since the 8th century. Defining your hara allows you to develop a better appreciation of your self. It takes you to the very core of your self; it is a way of experiencing who you are in a fundamental way.

Usui taught what follows, Makoto No Kokyu - the breath of truth - to his First Degree students as they moved towards Second Degree level, and it was only when they had worked with this exercise for some time that they moved on to Second Degree. The exercise itself is not the easiest of exercises to Master, but like all things it becomes easier with practice. Makoto No Kokyu can be seen as consisting of three distinct phases:

1. Introduction
2. Golden Ki Flow
3. Hara Defining

1. Introduction – do this once

1. Sit in Seiza (or more likely on a sofa or cross-legged on the floor) with your hands palms down on your knees, and close your eyes
2. Begin to observe your breathing; follow your in- and out-breaths for a little while, until your mind becomes calm.
3. Open your eyes slightly and focus your attention on a point on the wall or the floor about 3 ft (86 cm) in front of you.

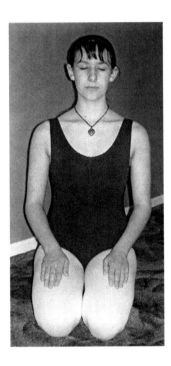

2. Golden Ki Flow – do this once

1. As you breathe in, visualise Ki entering your body as a golden flow from all around you
2. Be aware of the energy as it flows through your body and fills your hara
3. With each out breath flood the golden energy out of your body in all directions and witness the flow of Ki engulfing your surroundings in golden energy
4. Do this for at least ten in-breath/out-breath sequences

3. Defining the Hara - repeat this sequence

1. Move your hands into the Gassho position, with your hands in front of your chest in the sort of position where you could breathe out onto your fingertips
2. Part your hands slightly, keeping the index finger and thumb tips still in contact with each other
3. Move your hands down to the solar plexus
4. Imagine "Golden Ki Flow" coming to and from your hara for three complete breaths

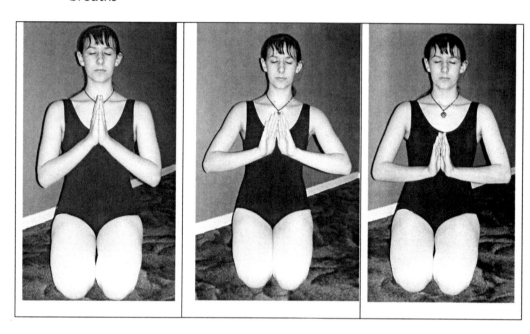

5. On the in-breath, bring the hands up to the brow, forming the sign of the sun

171

6. With the next out-breath of Golden Ki, sound out the jumon/kotodama "On" (the Japanese version of "Om") and as you do this bring your hands/arms down so that your fingertips are touching the floor/settee; this takes as long as your breath

7. Leave your fingers in contact with the floor for a few moments

8. Move your hands to the abdomen beneath the navel, with your left hand overlapping your right hand

9. Feel the vibration of Ki within your hara; you might want to stay in this position for a little while before moving on, to experience your hara for longer, or for the location and dimensions of your hara to become more apparent to you

10. Now go back to stage 1 of the "Defining the Hara" section and repeat this sequence at least ten times. Do **NOT** go back to repeat the 'Introduction' and 'Golden Ki Flow' sections.

The sound 'On' is made quite nasally, like the French 'nnn' sound.

Important note

In the original instructions you are supposed to intone "On" when breathing in, which is a very good trick if you can do it!!

A second best is to chant 'On' on the out-breath, and Chris Marsh told me that it probably wouldn't make much difference, so I have framed the instructions in terms of chanting on the out-breath rather than the in-breath. But do have a go at chanting on the in-breath if you wish.

Makoto No Kokyu, Part Two

Once students had fully defined their hara, there was a further stage to be carried out, which could have been appended onto the sequence above on occasion, but was mostly used on its own. Here it is...

1. Sit in Seiza, with your hands palms down on your knees, and close your eyes
2. Visualise your hara
3. When your hara has been located/experienced, breathe naturally and imagine golden Ki entering your nose and filling your hara
4. On the out-breath visualise the exhaled Ki filling the room with golden light
5. Repeat the in-breaths and out-breaths for 10-15 minutes before physical work, mental work, or energy work

Buddhist-style meditations

There were two methods used by Usui Sensei's students to experience the energies of earth ki and heavenly ki, and to experience a state of oneness. Some students chanted kotodama in order to experience these energies, and some used Buddhist-style meditations; that is what I want to talk about here. Once the students had worked with each meditation for several months, they would be given the corresponding kotodama, which elicited the energy or state that they had already been experiencing through meditation.

Which approach was used depended on the need of the student. Buddhist students were more likely to be given meditations first, while Shinto followers were more likely to be given the kotodama straight away, to chant and meditate upon.

Chi No Kokyu - the breath of earth

Here are the instructions for carrying out this exercise.

1. Sit in seiza if you can (see below). If not, sit cross-legged with your spine erect.
2. Close your eyes and rest your hands in your lap, palms up. Your left hand rests on top of your right hand and your thumb-tips touch gently.
3. Experience the sensation of your body in contact with the earth.
4. Exhale forcefully (see below). Feel the energy of your body merge with the earth. Pause before breathing in, and during that time allow your body to feel itself merging with earth energy.
5. Breathe in naturally.
6. Go back to point 4 and repeat, so that you have carried out five forceful exhalations.

You may carry this out several times a day, and this exercise is very useful to help you with grounding, if you feel that you need to be grounded.

The forceful exhalation that you carry out has been described by Hiroshi Doi as "Hado breathing". You breathe out through your mouth, making a "Haaaaa" sound, as if you are feeling relieved. Do not force this; take your time with the exhalation. Vibrate the sound throughout your mouth.

This exercise would have been carried out for at least six months before the student moved on to experience the energy of heavenly ki.

Seiza

Here is a line drawing to illustrate the 'seiza' sitting position.

174

Ten No Kokyu - the breath of heaven

Here are the instructions for carrying out this exercise.

1. Sit in seiza if you can. If not, sit cross-legged with your spine erect.
2. Close your eyes and breathe normally to calm your mind. Your hands are resting palms down on your knees.
3. When you feel ready, exhale firmly (not Hado breathing!) and bring your hands into Gassho position, with your left thumb crossed over your right thumb.
4. Breathe in and, with your hands still together, raise your hands above your crown. Feel Ki entering your body through the crown as you inhale.
5. Breathe out through your nose and, as you do so, bring your hands down in a circular movement and join them again in front of your heart in the Gassho position. You are tracing the 'egg' of the etheric body.
6. As the breath is exhaled, feel your body merging with the essence of heaven. Embrace the feelings of universal peace and knowledge.
7. Go back to point 4 and repeat, so you have carried out a maximum of ten in- and out-breaths.

This exercises is said to unite your body and mind with cosmic energy and understanding.

The Ki that emanates from heaven is light, passive and etherical (that is, it relates to the etheric body). Heavenly Ki is golden in colour.

This exercise would have been carried out for at least six months before the student moved on to experience a state of oneness, something that only a minority of Usui Sensei's Second Degree students went on to do.

Jin No Kokyu - the breath of being

Here are the instructions for carrying out this exercise, which is used to elicit a state of oneness, or an understanding of oneness, in the student.

1. Sit in seiza if you can. If not, sit cross-legged with your spine erect.
2. Close your eyes and rest your hands in your lap, palms up. Your left hand rests on top of your right hand and your thumb-tips touch gently.
3. Observe your breathing and how it feels. Be aware of its life-giving power.
4. Continue observing your normal, gentle breathing for several minutes.
5. If your mind wanders, you can bring your attention back by gently refocusing on your breathing.
6. As you breathe in, say to yourself in your mind: "Breath is life".
7. As you breathe out, say to yourself in your mind: "Life is breath".
8. Repeat these affirmations for as long as you can without being distracted.

Suwari Kokkyu ho - seated Ki breathing

This exercise was carried out by students who were preparing to commence their Shinpiden training with Usui Sensei. The exercise is in two parts. In the first part the student brings themselves into alignment with earth ki. Having done this, the student moves on to experience heavenly ki, then blending the two energies within them.

Part 1: Earth ki

1. Sit in seiza if you can. If not, sit cross-legged with your spine erect.
2. Your hands are resting palms down on your thighs with your fingers pointing towards your knees.
3. Close your eyes and breathe normally to calm your mind. Observe your breathing for a time.
4. Visualise and feel earth ki entering your body through your knees with each in-breath and circulating in your Tanden, filling you with strength and power. Earth ki is forest green in colour, heavy, firm and powerful.
5. Imagine that each green in-breath aligns you with earth.
6. Breathe out through your nose, your breath filling the room with green ki.
7. Go back to point 4 and repeat, so that you have carried out ten in-breaths and out-breaths.
8. You are now grounded by your link with Earth ki.

Part 2: combined Earth ki and Heavenly ki

1. Open your eyes and focus on a point three feet in front of you. Breathe normally for a short while.
2. Move your hands to your sides with your fingers loosely outstretched.
3. Breathe in through your nose. As you do so, rise up on your knees and raise your hands to shoulder level.
4. Experience the golden heavenly ki travelling to the Tanden and blending with the green earth ki.
5. As your lungs become full, raise your hands into the sign on the sun above your head.
6. Hold your breath for a few seconds and feel the lightness of heavenly ki.
7. As you exhale, bring your arms back to your sides and lower yourself back into seiza.
8. As you do so, visualise the green and the gold of the combined ki leaving your body and filling the room with a gold and green cloud, making you feel invincible, as you experience the joining of heaven and earth.
9. Go back to point 3 and repeat, so that you have carried out ten in-breaths and out-breaths.

As you practice, you will find that the golden heavenly ki will become more prominent until a point of harmony is reached between the two energies.

Master Level meditations

The Energy-Ball Self-empowerment

This method was taught by Usui to his Master students so that they could, in effect, attune themselves at Master level each day (though using the word 'attune' is a little inappropriate!). The method involves the creation of an energy ball between your hands, which is empowered by chanting the empowerment kotodama, the ball then being drawn into your heart and down to your Tanden. The technique can be added onto the end of Hatsurei ho, or can be carried out after performing kenyoku/joshin kokkyu ho. I recommend that you carry out this exercise daily, and if you do this then do not be surprised if you experience a 'clear-out' on some level. Here are the instructions:

1. Perform Hatsurei ho in the normal way (or perform Kenyoku/Joshin Kokkyu ho). When you have completed the Seishin Toitsu stage of Hatsurei, imagine that an energy ball is building up between your hands, which are in Gassho.*

2. Allow your hands to drift apart as the energy ball gets bigger. Imagine that the ball is filling with energy, becoming stronger and more intense.

3. Intone the empowerment kotodama three times (preferably out loud), with the intention that the energy ball fills with the empowerment energy.

4. Allow the energy ball to get stronger and stronger.

5. Now breathe the energy into your body, pulling the energy first into your heart. The way that I do this is to allow my hands to drift away from my body so that they are facing my chest and, as I inhale, I **push** the energy ball into my heart and rest my hands one over the other on my chest. Feel the energy in your heart for as long as you like: take your time. Don't rush this.

6. Then pull the energy down to your Tanden, and feel the energy there. I move my hands down the front of my body so that they rest one over the other in front of my Tanden, imagining that the energy is moving from the heart to the Tanden in time with my hand movements. Feel the energy in your Tanden for as long as you like: take your time. Don't rush this.

7. Finish Hatsurei ho in the normal way.

* Note: If you are carrying out Kenyoku/Joshin Kokkyu ho, then when you are ready simply move your hands into Gassho and follow the instructions above.

I am able to share a couple more Master level meditations with you, informally, assuming that you carry out the energy-ball self-empowerment regularly. I suggest that you carry out the energy-ball self-empowerment most days for 6 months and we can take it from there.

Microcosmic Orbit Meditation

This meditation has nothing to do with Reiki, really, and is a modification of an energy practice from Qi Gong. Many things have been added into Reiki over the years from various sources, and this is a practice that is passed on in some lineages but not all. Simon Treselyan wrote the information and descriptions below...

"Any meditation is best if done regularly, and the Reiki meditation is no exception to this. It can be done simply whenever time allows. Remember however that finding the time is often an important act of discipline that enriches the act of meditation. The exercise combines the benefit of normal transcendental and other meditations, with the healing powers of Reiki. Regular use will enhance healing, psychic powers, create relaxation and harmony, and clarify the visualisation process of the individual. The meditation is an excellent medium for empowering, and thereby achieving goals, and problem solving. The meditation is in three parts.

Simplified version

First, though, here is a more straightforward version of the meditation, which my first Reiki Teacher, Diane Whittle taught me, during my Master course. It puts to one side the goal-manifesting part of the meditation and concentrates on sending Reiki energy through the 'microcosmic orbit'. Enjoy the sensations. Here it is:

1   *Sit quietly. Try putting the Antahkarana symbol (male or female) under your feet. Close your eyes and breathe slowly and deeply.*
2   *imagine a shaft of brilliant white light entering your crown chakra from above and feel the sensation for a little while. Then visualise the Usui Master symbol as if it were on a vast screen in front of you. Visualise in violet and look at the symbol for a few moments. Empower the symbol by saying its name three times. Then visualise the symbol moving upwards into this field of light above your head.*
3   *repeat the process with the Tibetan Master symbol.*
4   *repeat the process with the Distant symbol.*
5   *repeat the process with the Mental/Emotional symbol.*
6   *repeat the process with the Power symbol.*
7   *hold all the symbols above your crown chakra.*
8   *Contract your Huiyin and put your tongue to the roof of your mouth.*
9   *imagine the Reiki symbols and their associated energy passing slowly into your crown chakra. Hold it there for a little while and notice any sensation.*
10   *slowly move the energy round to the third eye chakra and hold it there for a while. Notice any sensation. I found at this point that I could feel a burning, tingling, fizzing, gnawing sensation.*
11   *Continue to move the energy round the circuit shown in the diagram, stopping at each point for a while, and then moving on.*
12   *once you have completed three slow circuits, imagine a continuous flow of energy round and round the circuit, for as long as you wish.*
13   *finally, seal each of your seven chakras with a power symbol and then your whole body with a large one.*

Microcosmic Orbit Diagram

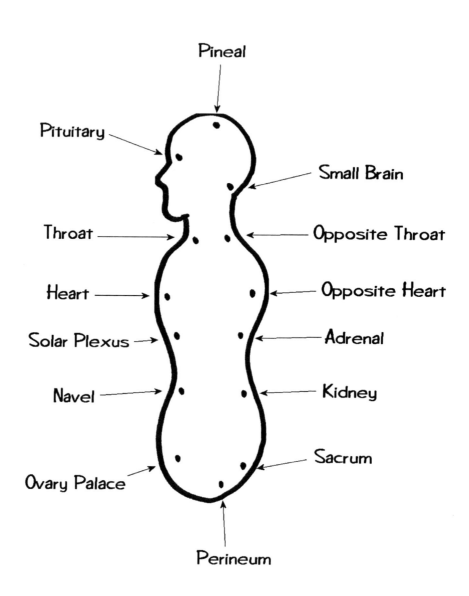

Part One of the Longer Meditation

1 Sit quietly in a chair with your hands either on the heart chakra, or placed loosely in the lap. Close your eyes and breathe slowly and deeply, thinking of Reiki.

2 Draw the Usui Master symbol in front of you, visualising it in violet light, and retain the image for several minutes. As other thoughts come into your mind, allow them to pass on by and return to the image. Practice will allow the image to be retained for longer periods without interruption. For those who have difficulties in visualising, it may be useful to draw the symbol on paper and concentrate on it between periods of retaining the image in thought-form.

3 Chant the sacred name of the symbol three times, aloud if no one will be within earshot.

4 Visualise the symbol moving upwards into a field of light above your crown chakra.

5 Repeat the process with the Distant symbol.

6 Repeat the process with the Mental/Emotional symbol.

7 Repeat the process with the Power symbol.

Part Two - Manifesting Goals

8 Meditate on the problem or goal to be achieved. Give it a name and visualise the goal or problem in its completed and positive sense.

9 State the goal or problem to be achieved out loud. Visualise your image now surrounded by the four Reiki symbols. Continue with this visualisation for several minutes, and use will and intent to create the image of accomplishment.

10 Repeat this process with any other goal or problem.

11 When the visualisation is complete, state "If this be possible within Divine Love and Wisdom, So mote it be!" Then believe that the process has been successfully completed.

12 Relax and allow the subject to leave your conscious mind.

13 To fully complete the meditation, place the tongue to the roof of the mouth and allow your conscious mind to concentrate on the 'Hara' centre - the solar plexus.

14 Draw the Power symbol in front of you with the spiral at the Hara centre, and pat the area three times to release any build-up of energy. Chant the sacred name of the Power symbol three times.

15 Hold you attention at the Hara centre for approximately ten minutes to allow the energies to balance within the mind and body.

16 Breathe slowly and open your eyes.

This is an excellent meditation for the empowering of crystals, especially if you will be using the crystals in conjunction with a Reiki grid. Remember that any such meditation is only as powerful as the will and intent that is put into it.

Part Three

Place the Antahkarana symbol under the feet, then after step #13 above, continue...

14   Picture the power symbol at the navel point and hold the attention there for between 30 seconds to a few minutes.
15   Move to the next point down (see diagram) and do the same.
16   Work up the spine and down the front to the navel, to open and clear each chakra.
17   Send white light around this circuit for several minutes, through each point.
18   Seal the chakras with the power symbol. Seal the whole body with the Power symbol.

The purpose of this part is to open and clear the chakras to allow higher energies to be used, and to prevent problems caused by too much energy in the head or other parts. Circulating the energy will purify and release any negative energy within the body. This is a modified form of the Taoist microcosmic orbit meditation. It is very soothing and creates a calm and balanced state.

Lotus Repentance Meditation

The Lotus Repentance meditation is not an essential part of original Usui Reiki. It was not part of the daily practice of Masters, though they were encouraged to carry out the meditation at some stage during their Master training. The meditation comes from Tendai Buddhism.

The purpose of this meditation is to bring satori, or a moment of enlightenment, and it is the framework for the practice that Usui carried out on Mount Kurama. This meditation, in its full form, is not for the fainthearted. It involves 21 days of fasting and meditating, and nobody really carries this out nowadays in Japan: they are all too busy and it is for the brave or foolhardy. Usui is said to have carried out the full 21-day meditation five times during his lifetime.

So I have included this meditation for information only. It would have started in a meditation hall at the foot of the mountain, where you would make vows, ritual movements, and chant phrases containing kotodama. You would find a spot on the mountain to meditate, and at sunset you would return to the meditation hall and carry out further rituals. This would continue for 21 days, so Usui did not disappear up a mountain, to return 21 days later with Reiki; that is another fable that has come to us from Mrs Takata.

What follows is a shortened version of the meditation that Usui would have carried out; maybe a handful of people in Japan might still know the original version. The version below is sanctioned by the Tendai Monks at Mt Hiei.

I do not suggest that you try to carry out this meditation; it is included in the manual for information only.

Zazen Shikan Taza (The meditation used by Usui)

Outside the meditation hall or spiritual practice area

1   Shikan Zen Yo No Ichi Ge

the verse displaying the main point of samatha-vipasyana meditation

Recite once:

"In the genuine entering nirvana, apparently there are a multitude of roads. But if we think about only the vital necessities, two practice methods stand out. The first, samatha, quiets one's evil passions, and the second, vipasyana, further leads one to deny unwholesome desires. When samatha results in one's winning entry into dhyana-samadhi, then vipasyana becomes the foundation of prajna. When both samatha and vipasyana are successfully practised, the meditator enters samadhi and receives prajna. In that state, the dharma's altruistic goal of helping both self and others is fully completed."

Notes:

Samatha	*stopping, ceasing all activity*
Dhyana-Samadhi	*meditation trance*
Vipasyana	*insight*
Prajna	*wisdom*
Dharma	**the path/truth**

2   Kokoro No Ryo

verse on food for the heart/mind

Recite once each:

"Practising the dharma includes food and clothes, but in food and clothes the practice of dharma is not found."

"Monetary wealth is not a national treasure; a person who brightens a single corner is a national treasure."

"The height of compassion is to welcome evil onto myself while giving good deeds to other people, and to forget myself while doing good for others."

"By holding grudges and repaying with hatred, hatred never ends; but by repaying with virtue, hatred is completely exhausted. Rather than bearing grudges about the things happening in this long night's dream called the world, cross the boundary into the dharma realm of the true Buddha."

3   the Sange Mon

Line up outside the hall.

Recite the Sange Mon (repentance verse) once:

"Ga Shaku Sho Zo Sho Aku Go, Kai Yu Mu Shi Ton Jin Chi, Ju Shin Go I Shi Sho Sho, Issai Ga Kon Kai Sange"

Translation: From beginningless time I have generated negative karma through my misdirected thoughts, words and deeds. I wish to acknowledge and atone for all.

Enter the hall...

Inside the meditation hall or spiritual practice area

4   San Rai

three prostrations

Recite three times, each time performing a grand prostration after each recitation:

"Isshin Chorai Jippo Hokai Joju Sanbo"

Translation: I the penitent come to make amends for my transgressions

Great Prostration: Stand in gassho, then move into the kneeling position with hands in Gassho, then lay on ground face down with hands straight out in front of you

5   Ten non-virtuous states of mind

the recitation on self-discipline

This is done individually. Contemplate:

Reflecting on my own life, I should abandon those heart-states in which bad actions accumulate, namely the realms of hells, animals, hungry ghosts, fighting entities, mundane life, heavens, evil spirits, Hinayana followers, professional priests, and conflicting emotions.

6   Godai Gan

five great vows

Recite:

"Shujo Muhen Segan Do
Fukuchi Muhen Segan Shu
Homon Muhen Segan Gaku
Nyorai Muhen Segan Ji
Mujo Bodai Segan Jo
Goji Busshi Jodaigan"

Translation:

Sentient beings are limitless, I vow to save them all.
Knowledge and wisdom are limitless, I vow to accumulate them all.
The dharmas are infinite, I vow to study them all.
The tathagatas are endless, I vow to serve them all.
Supreme enlightenment is unsurpassed. I vow to attain it.
May this seeker of enlightenment fulfil these vows.

Note: The **Tathagata** means the accomplished one, an enlightened being, like a buddha. There are ten levels of bodhisattvaship until you reach the state of a buddha with the complete realisation of emptiness and compassion. The buddha himself had several incarnations as a bodhisattva (a being that is completely motivated by the wish to help others and no more interested in anything for himself), before he became the buddha.

Take your seat for meditation...

7 Entering samadhi

First, check one's posture. If sitting in the half-lotus position, place the left leg over the right leg. Pull it close to the body, with the left toes and the right heel equally spaced. Loosen the belt and arrange the clothes neatly so as to cover the legs. Form the meditation mudra with the hands in the lap, right palm on top of the left palm, with the tips of the thumbs lightly touching, pulled close under the stomach. Twist the body left and right a number of times, coming to rest in a correct, straight posture. The backbone should not be curved, and the shoulders are thrown back. If the posture should relax, without hurrying, quickly correct it.

Clear the air passages, expelling muddy spirits. Exhale with the mouth open, releasing stagnant air slowly while leaning slightly forward. Don't exhale quickly or slowly, but continue until you are satisfied. Breathe all defects out during exhalation, completely exhausting them. Then straighten up again, and through the nose breathe in endless, pure spirit. Imagine it entering through the top of the head, in and out three times.

Then with the torso straight and relaxed, allow the diaphragm to move in tandem with the movement of air through the nose. Close the mouth, teeth lightly together, tongue against the upper palate. With the eyes half-closed to reduce the brightness of the outside light, let the line of sight fall about six feet in front.

Second, check the breathing. Listening to the sound of the in- and out-breaths, it should not be loud, not gasping or sucking in air, not jerky, puckering or sliding. Allow the breathing to remain in a natural state, as if in a closed system.

Third, check the activity of the thoughts. Separate the attention from the breathing and concentrate it at the red field. Abandon those thoughts outside the practice, such as gross thoughts, random thoughts, day dreaming, thoughts about emotional ups and downs, or relaxed and tense states.

Note: the red field is what you can see when you half close your eyelids and turn your eyes upwards.

8 Dwelling in samadhi

Observe the harmony of the Three Mysteries of the body, the breath and the thoughts. Note when the three are not in harmony, and continually apply mindfulness and recollection to again produce unity and harmony of the body, breath and thoughts. Rely on this practice to cross over. One sits single-pointedly, not being shaken by thoughts or activities of daily life, not even if enveloped in raging flames.

185

9   Exiting samadhi

First, release the mind from samadhi, and establish connections and relations. Next, open the mouth and breathe deeply so as to release the spirit. Next, move the body very slightly. Then move the hands, down over the arms with a sweeping motion from shoulder to fingertip (a la kenyoku), then returning the hand back up the arm, from the elbow to the shoulder and on over the neck, head, the neck and shoulder on the other side, finishing with a flourishing flick as you remove negative energy. Do the same with the other hand. Next, rub the pores of the whole body (rub your forearms), then rub the palms together, using warmth to cover the eyes. Next, open the eyes behind the palms. Finally, light incense or recite sutras depending on the time.

10   Method for leaving the hall

If there is time, recite sutras. This can be the Heart sutra, the Ten-verse Kannon sutra, portions of the Lotus sutra, the sutra of Saintly Fudo, or any other sutra you choose. You may also chant the Nembutsu and dedicate merit.

Finally, recite the San Rai (three prostrations) again, three times, each time performing a Grand Prostration.

"Isshin Chorai Jippo Joju Sanbo"

Depart the hall...

Note; the reason why it is required to recite some sections in Japanese is that these passages contain kotodama within them, and they produce particular effects.

Miscellaneous Western Techniques

Master Course Audio CD Number 1 - track #8

Reiki 'Psychic Surgery'

This Reiki version of 'psychic surgery' is something that I have never carried out myself. To me it seems a very cumbersome set of rituals that serve only to focus your intent, and I think that focusing one's intent can be done in ways that are not anything like so complicated as the descriptions presented in the following paragraphs.

I have done what might be called 'informal psychic surgery', where I have used small hand movements mimicking the removal of an object or 'block', and for me that is sufficient. When I have done this, it has been an intuitive practice, making the hand movements when it seems to be the right thing to do, going with the flow. So I believe that we should use our intuition in terms of where we place our hands (Reiji Ho), what symbols (or kotodama) we should use (what aspects of the energy we emphasise) and also what particular hand movements we make, if any.

Here is the information that was passed on to me...

> "Psychic surgery is a technique to remove deep-rooted blocks of negativity that can be hampering a person's progress. These blockages are often the root cause of disease and if not dealt with effectively can cause great anguish and instability."

> "Such negativity can collect around individual organs and chakras, effectively strangulating their growth. Psychic surgery is a very effective way of dealing with these negative aspects of life, and can be beneficial in the alleviating of physical, emotional or health problems."

Instructions

It is usual to conduct Reiki psychic surgery after a healing attunement and before a normal Reiki session.

Firstly, the person to be healed must want the problem taken away, and therefore it relies on their total co-operation. It is imperative that the practitioner spends some time with the client assessing the problem.

The client should be seated comfortably. Then ask the person to describe the condition to be healed. Ask the client to meditate on the condition, and ask them where in the body they believe the condition to be residing. This would not necessarily be in the obvious position. Migraines caused by stress may have their root in the emotional chakra around the heart for example. The client will know best where they feel the condition is seated.

Next ask the client to identify a shape, colour, texture, weight, even smell, of the condition to be removed. Thus identified, both the practitioner, using his/her intuition, and the client, using feeling, can assess any shift in the negative energy. The client then needs to actively meditate on letting go of the blockage, creating a willingness to learn and assimilate any knowledge or lesson gained from the experience.

1. Say a silent prayer, asking for the help of your spiritual guides and the Reiki guides.

2. Silently state that this is to be Reiki Psychic surgery.

3. Draw the Usui Master symbol and the Power symbol on your palms.

4. Draw the Power symbol on each chakra and over the whole body, to empower and open yourself.

5. Draw all six Reiki symbols in the air, intending their power to fill the room. Visualise the symbols in violet as if on a great screen in the middle of the room, and say their names three times, mantra-style, to empower them. Use this order... Tibetan Master, Fire Serpent, Usui Master, Distant, Mental/Emotional, Power.

6. With a firm will and intent, pull your fingers, visualising them extend to about nine inches. Take an in-breath during this process, and repeat it twice.

7. Draw the Power symbol over the ends of the visualised fingers and tap them three times.

8. Draw the Mental/Emotional symbol over the area identified and tap the area three times. Cover with the Power symbol.

9. Stand in a balanced but strong position and focus your will and intent on the area. When ready, using your full inner strength, push the visualised Reiki fingers into the area; it does not matter if the physical fingers make contact or not. Visualise the fingers gripping the shape and withdraw them with a powerful intake of breath.

10. Bring your hands to your mouth and blow the negativity, with a short powerful breath, upward to divine source where it can be dispersed. This must be done with the full force of your being.

11. Repeat this process for 3-5 minutes. It is important to breathe the negative energy out of the hands, so as not to draw any of the substance into yourself. Use your intuition to see which is the best way to extricate the shape from the body. It is usual to actually feel the shift in the client as this process is carried out. Remember: if it feels right, do it! You may well wish to attempt the process from different positions.

12. Ask the client to concentrate on the area concerned and report any changes in feeling. The shape may have decreased, or moved, or even disappeared altogether. If the shape remains in any form, repeat the process until the client reports that the negative feeling has gone. There are times when several attempts do not entirely shift the negativity.

13. In this case, draw the Mental/Emotional symbol, tapping the area three times, followed by the Power symbol in similar fashion. Silently ask the area what further treatment or lesson needs to be learnt before the condition can be removed.

14. Ask the client to report any image or communication he or she feels, irrespective of how relevant it seems on an intellectual basis. You too must trust and say the first thing felt or received.

15. Armed with further knowledge you will know whether the condition can be relieved in the session or not. It may be that an alternative way of letting go is required. It may take forgiveness or further affirmation.

16. Continue with the surgery, if appropriate, shifting the energy therein. It is possible that further sessions are necessary to adequately shift the negativity. However, the healing power will continue to work long after the surgery has taken place.

17. After finishing the surgery, place your hands over the treated area and allow Reiki to flow, sealing it with the Power symbol and tapping the area three times.

18. Take a definite step backwards away from the client and 'chop' the link between yourselves. This is a positive affirmation that you will not take on any of the client's negativity under any circumstances.

19. Retract your Reiki fingers as you blow air out, again sealing the ends with the Power symbol and tapping them three times.

Now continue with a standard Reiki treatment.

Reiki and Crystals

You have already read about Usui's use of crystals, in conjunction with the kotodama. Below you can read about a Western use of crystals. I am not really 'into' crystals, so I have not pursued this technique.

Simon Treselyan wrote this section...

Distant Healing using Crystals

You will already be familiar with distant healing, which is taught in Reiki II. Here is a technique for facilitating the projection of the energy by the use of crystals...

1   Obtain a photograph of the person to be healed, and choose a cleansed crystal to be used for the healing. This may be normal rock quartz, or may be the birthstone of the person.

2   Place the crystal over the photograph and draw the Distant, Master and Power symbols over them, visualising the symbol in violet and saying each symbol name three times.

3   Hold the photograph and crystal together and project the healing energy towards the person to be healed.

4   Place the photograph and crystal in a secure place where it will not be disturbed.

The crystal will continue to transmit the energy to the person. The crystal will need to be charged every day for the first three days, then the crystal will need to be charged every 42 - 72 hours to maintain the energy.

Creating and using a 'Reiki Grid'

By employing a crystal Reiki Grid one can continue to send Reiki or empower goals for long periods if the grid is charged. The grid itself, when used, becomes multidimensional and allows a link to your higher self and Reiki guides to transmit healing and knowledge.

The grid uses eight crystals, one of which will be a 'master' crystal. Although any crystals will do in theory, rock quartz is best in practice. The crystals will have to be cleansed with rock or sea salt and pure water. Sun or moon 'bathing' is also useful to cleanse the energy of the crystal. The crystals will need to be 'charged' with Reiki before they can be used, and for this the Reiki meditation (part two) will suffice.

The grid will have to be set up in a sacred space away from casual inspection or interference, and will be placed on an Antahkarana.

You will need to choose a master crystal, preferably one that is easily held in one hand. The crystal should be male in energy since it will be used to focus the Reiki energy. The six normal crystals are placed on the outer hexagon facing inwards towards the central crystal, which should hold special significance. It has been found that a crystal ball, pyramid or cluster harnesses the Reiki energy well. Once you have the configuration that feels right, affix the crystals with a small piece of adhesive to prevent the crystals from moving.

The crystals will now need to be charged with Reiki and know their purpose as part of the grid. Reiki the crystals for about 10 minutes each whilst tuning in to your individual guides for increased purity. You can if you wish attune the crystal to the Reiki energy. Place each individual crystal on its place within the grid, placing the centre crystal last. Charge the master crystal last in exactly the same way as the others.

The master-crystal will become a part of your Reiki life and therefore has to be special to each Master. As an integral part of the grid, it is used to charge it, and keep it charged.

To charge the grid, hold the master crystal in your dominant hand and point it downward at the central crystal. Begin to draw out triangular sections on the grid, starting at the centre, moving out to one of the six crystals, and then across anticlockwise to the next, and back to the centre. Continue to perform this around the grid whilst intoning a mantra-like affirmation, filling the grid with Light, Love, Peace, Wisdom, affirming all the words three times. An example would be "I charge this grid with Reiki, with Reiki, with Reiki, to Heal, to Heal, to Heal." Continue with this process until you feel that the positive affirmations have filled the grid. At first you will find it difficult to create the rhythm and you may miss a few lines. Speed will come with practice, and you will quickly find that the mantras aid in adding a flowing charging motion. The grid must continue to be charged every 2-3 days since crystals have only a finite power. The more you work the grid, the greater the results obtained.

The master crystal will become a close friend and an excellent meditation tool, enhancing awareness and sensitivity. Powerful results will be attained if the crystal is charged with the Reiki meditation, and then used to activate the grid.

Absent charging

There may be occasions when you are separated from the grid but wish to continue to use it for empowerment. In this case it is useful to carry a photograph of the made-up grid which can be activated by your master crystal in exactly the same way. If you are doing this, first apply the distance symbol, charge the grid, and empower it with the Power symbol. Such distant charging will maintain the grid's powers indefinitely.

Use of the grid

To use the grid for the empowering of goals or the healing of an individual, you will need to write out exactly what is required of the grid, and place it in the centre, being careful not to disturb the centre crystal. Be careful what you ask for since you may just get it! For absent healing books, open the book and stand it on end in the grid. Energy will be sent to all within.

Use of the grid requires responsibility since it is very powerful. I personally used the grid for recovery of my car, which had been stolen. The car was found and returned to me within 24 hours! It is always advisable to affirm when charging the grid "If this be possible within divine love and wisdom, so mote it be".

The Antahkarana

The antahkarana has nothing to do with Usui Reiki and - along with the 'Tibetan' Master symbol and the Fire Dragon - were introduced into Western Reiki by an American man called Arthur Robertson, who died in 2001 I believe. I do not use Antahkaranas myself, but I have included them in this manual for completeness.

Simon Treselyan wrote this section...

The Antahkarana is a part of our spiritual anatomy connecting the physical and higher selves, which is the necessary balance to grow spiritually. It is based on Radionics which indicates that the space around the lines drawn on paper creates an energy that has a direct effect on the human psyche. Used in China and Tibet for thousands of years, the Antahkarana is a very ancient healing and meditation symbol. The symbol has a consciousness of its own and will work independently of the practitioner's energy. However, when actively used in healing it focuses the energy used and produces a Taoist microcosmic orbit creating an energy flow up the governor channel and down the functional channel. This continuous energy flow grounds and cleanses the body while activating the chakras.

The Antahkarana can be used in a variety of ways to enhance all forms of healing disciplines. The symbol itself is multidimensional and when first looked at appears as a two dimensional form of three 7s within a circle. These represent the seven colours of the rainbow, seven notes of the musical scale, and seven chakras. From a Christian viewpoint the three sevens are significant in representing the Book of Revelations testament to seven trumpets, candlesticks, and seals. As a three-dimensional object the symbol appears as a cube. Continued use as a meditation tool will allow the practitioner to experience further dimensional possibilities as the Antahkarana's unseen dimensions rise towards the higher self.

The history of the symbol is sketchy but it is widely held that it was a sacred meditation tool known to very few masters. The symbol is unlikely to have originated in Tibet, although no records exist. Again channellers are divided in their perceptions as to the symbol's origin. The symbol does indeed work and that is its own validity. It is thought that the original Tibetan meditation practice was carried out in a candle-lit room. A large earthenware oval bowl was filled with several inches of water, representing the cosmic and the waters of life. In the centre of the egg, a stool with the Antahkarana inlaid in silver was placed. A copper polished wall was in front of the person creating a natural mirror; behind the person were hung tapestries depicting the

Reiki symbols. Meditation was then carried out on the symbols creating a focused consciousness, allowing this to unite with the energies of the symbols. The Antahkarana symbol on the stool focused the energies created into a steady flow within the person.

The Antahkarana is a high intensity production of nan-o-ray energy for use in cellular regeneration and toxic remission. It produces energy in the shape of a flame, with a spike of energy in the centre, which is the strongest point within the field. A large unit will produce a large field. The Antahkarana contains the acoustical frequencies of white light. The energy flame of white light can be measured with an electron counter. The white light flame moves in a clockwise spin, thereby restoring diseased cells' anticlockwise spin.

Uses of the Antahkarana

The Antahkarana works directly on the subtle bodies and the effects will vary with the needs of the individual. The symbol cannot cause harm since it works directly through the higher self.

- Objects placed between two symbols will be cleansed of negative energy.

- Symbols placed under massage tables (three is the most effective), or chairs, will have a very positive effect on the healing power of most therapies.

- Lying upon the symbols for three minutes can reverse body magnetic poles and body polarity, which results in chakra balance. When the body is exposed to the symbol, transmutation of disease can take place.

- If the energy needs to be concentrated on a small spot, use one of the corners of the symbol and press it on the area for three minutes.

- Photographs can be placed on the symbol to aid distant healing: place the photograph down three times on the symbol and leave it there for a minimum of three days, since three is the number of transmutation.

- Water can be purified in nine minutes by placing it on an Antahkarana. Plutonium, lead, copper, mercury, radon and radioactive contamination will be removed. Since the human body is mainly composed of water, the symbols work in the same way upon the body.

Meditation using the Antahkarana

The Antahkarana is a valuable tool for meditation, due to its multidimensional qualities.

Regular use of the symbol will give an inner clarity and a deeper, more profound result to the process.

Meditation is done by gazing directly but gently on the symbol, allowing any conscious thought to drift by.

As you begin to relax you will experience subtle shifts in the dimensional level of the symbol, and you may experience further visions or pictures within or covering the symbol.

The Antahkarana symbols

There are several variations of the Antahkarana symbol...

The Male symbol

This is the small Antahkarana symbol. Its use is primarily for direct healing since it has more focused and penetrating healing applications. Use the symbol as detailed in previous paragraphs.

The Female symbol

This is the larger single symbol and has a more gentle, nurturing, and general healing property. Its primary use would be under a therapy couch cover, or on a chair back, to increase the healing power, and create a relaxing effect.

The 'Cosmic Cross'

The cross consists of seven individual Antahkarana, corresponding to the chakras, in a line crossing each other. This symbol opens the heart to positive energy and purifies. Use the symbol directly on the heart chakra, placed face down.

The Square

The square is made up of sixteen individual symbols and is used to dispel negativity and blockages at any point in the body. It can release old congested thought forms and habits, and bring spontaneity back to life. Since the inherent property of the square is to dispel and scatter energy, it is advisable to ground the client afterwards. This can be achieved through meditation or by a direct application of the male symbol to the base chakra.

Appendix

Antahkaranas

THE ANTAHKARANA

THE MALE SYMBOL

THE ANTAHKARANA

THE FEMALE SYMBOL

THE ANTAHKARANA

THE COSMIC CROSS

THE ANTAHKARANA

THE SQUARE

Running Reiki Courses

 Master Course Audio CD Number 1 - track #12

The fact that you have become a Reiki Master/Teacher does not mean that you are now obliged to run courses and teach the general public; you do not need to run courses at all. Maybe you might decide to pass on the benefits of Reiki to some friends and family members in an informal way and go no further than that, and that's fine. But if you decide to move on to run formal Reiki training sessions then we have tried to make the process as easy as we can for you.

The first thing to remember about running your own courses is that Reiki is simple and you know far more about the subject than you realise. When you teach Reiki you are passing on a few practical skills, all skills that you have experience of using yourself. You have played around with energy and carried out Hatsurei, so you can show someone else how to do the same. You can help someone to get to grips with self-treatments: you have done loads of self-treatments. You can show someone how to give a Reiki treatment: you have done it yourself, so you can teach from a solid foundation of practical experience.

Below you can read about some resources that we have put together for you to help you with your courses and supporting your students:

1. Professionally printed course manuals
2. Audio CDs with commentary and guided meditations
3. An Internet support network for Reiki Evolution students to join
4. Distant empowerments for all Reiki people to tune into

In a separate manual, available only to Reiki Master Teachers who have trained with Reiki Evolution, we have put together a "Teaching Guide" containing course schedules and detailed descriptions, showing what to teach and how, for the three Reiki levels.

Reiki Course manuals

You don't need to put together your own course manual: you can use ours. If you have trained with Reiki Evolution at RMT level then current versions of all the Reiki Evolution course manuals are available to download for free. Just ask Taggart and he will arrange for you to receive a copy as a PDF file.

All the manuals are very big, though, and if you are going to try and print out copies for your students you are going to get through a huge amount of printer ink. This will cost quite a lot of money.

You will probably find it a lot easier to order copies of our manuals, which are professionally printed and bound and are available to all Reiki people to order, no matter what their lineage. If you visit our web site you can order individual copies, or you can order packs of four manuals at greatly discounted prices.

Manuals available are as follows

First Degree Manual
Second Degree Manual
Master/Teacher course Manual

Reiki Audio CDs.

The main points of what I say on each of the three courses are contained on the audio CDs, so they provide a useful way of revising the main areas of each course. Many teachers are sending the CDs out in advance to their students before they attend the day of their live training – as we do at Reiki Evolution. They are also using the CDs to play to their students during the course itself, both some of the commentary tracks and the guided meditations.

The CDs that are available are as follows:

1. First Degree commentary
2. Second Degree commentary
3. "Reiki Meditations" (hatsurei ho, self-treatment meditation, symbol meditation and distant healing session)
4. "Talking you through a Reiki treatment"
5. Master Course audio CDs (2 CDs: one with commentary and one with guided meditations and attunement/empowerment audio instructions)

If you visit our web site you can order the CDs individually or in packs (for example, you can order the first four CDs listed above for less than they cost individually).

If you have trained with Reiki Evolution then we can let you have the CDs for half price. Just ask Taggart and he will send you a link so that you can visit a special web page that is not accessible otherwise.

Internet support network for Reiki Evolution students to join.

If you have trained with Reiki Evolution then once your students have completed their Reiki course, I am happy for them to join the Reiki Evolution Internet support network so that they can keep in touch with other Reiki people and learn from the experiences of others. We host a social network where you can upload your photo, write blog posts, join in discussions and join various special interest groups, for example Reiki and Crystals, Reiki and Horses, Reiki and Paganism, Treating the Public, Master Teacher group, Distant Healing group etc. You can chat online with people in real time and make new friends. You can offer advice and ask questions.

If you have trained with Reiki Evolution than just send your students' names and e-mail addresses to Taggart (taggart@reiki-evolution.co.uk) and he will send them an invitation to join the group.

Here is part of a screen capture to show you how the support network looks. As you can see, new members are displayed at the top, with their photo if they have uploaded one. Below that you can see various special interest groups that people have decided to join. Each special interest group has its own message board. On the left you can see a slideshow of all the photos that members have uploaded, and below that you can see the latest blog posts

Below you can see further down the page. There are more blog posts on the left, and in the middle you can see various events listed. Below that is part of the main discussion board.

Distant Reiju empowerments for your students to tune in to.

I send out a Reiju empowerment, which any Reiki person can tune into any time on a Monday. Your students can tune into these distant empowerments too, no matter what your lineage is. They should carry out Hatsurei and then after Seishin Toitsu they should keep their hands in Gassho and say to themselves "I'm ready to receive my empowerment from Taggart now". They should then stay in Gassho until they feel that the empowerment has finished.

Alternatively, they could just carry out Kenyoku and Joshin Kokkyu ho, bring their hands into Gassho and say the same.

Alternatively they can simply get themselves comfortable in a chair, close their eyes, take a couple of deep breaths, bring their hands into Gassho and say the same.

Miscellaneous

Course Certificates

On the Reiki Evolution web site you can order Reiki certificates templates that you download them onto your computer. They are very simple, and are designed to be used in conjunction with 'certificate blanks' with pretty borders, which you can obtain from various stationers.

If you wish to design your own certificates then you can use Microsoft Publisher or Microsoft Word. You could print out a good quality original, and then have this original photocopied onto pretty marbled paper, available from craft or art supply shops, or onto certificate 'blanks'. You can then use your desktop printer to print out the student's name into the gap that you left on the certificate.

Business cards

You can obtain 250 business cards for free over the Internet; well, you pay the postage. You design them online and they are posted to you quite shortly afterwards.

Here is the site: www.vistaprint.co.uk

Reiki Leaflets

On the Reiki Evolution web site you can order Reiki leaflet templates on CD-ROM, or you can download them onto your computer. You can print out small quantities on your printer, or you can take one of the PDF files to your local printer for them to print out the leaflets in greater quantities.

Several leaflets are on the CD-ROM, promoting: Reiki treatments, Reiki courses, or both treatments and courses.

Recommended Books

If you are serious about setting yourself up as a Reiki teacher, then you need some advice about how to do this, how to promote Reiki and your courses. Here are some good books:

Getting Business to Come to You
Paul & Sarah Edwards and Laura Clampitt Douglas
Pub: Tarcher Putnam 1998

Get Clients Now!
C.J. Hayden
Pub: Amacom 1999

Guerrilla Marketing for the Home-Based Business
Jay Levinson & Seth Godin
Pub: Houghton Mifflin Company, New York

These books are also useful:

Business Mastery
Cherie M. Sohnen-Moe
Pub: Sohnen-Moe Associates Inc, 1988

Marketing for Complementary Therapists
Steven A. Harrold
Pub: howtobooks 200

Lightning Source UK Ltd.
Milton Keynes UK
11 February 2010

149877UK00001B/20/P